THE VIRUS IN THE AGE OF MADNESS

Bernard-Henri Lévy

Yale
UNIVERSITY PRESS
NEW HAVEN & LONDON

Yale University Press books may be purchased in quantity for educational, business, or promotional use. For information, please e-mail sales.press@yale.edu (U.S. office) or sales@yaleup.co.uk (U.K. office).

Printed in the United States of America.

Library of Congress Control Number: 2020939617
ISBN 978-0-300-25737-3 (paper : alk. paper)

A catalogue record for this book is available from the British Library.

This paper meets the requirements of ANSI/NISO Z39.48-1992 (Permanence of Paper).

THE VIRUS IN THE AGE OF MADNESS

ALSO BY BERNARD-HENRI LÉVY

The Empire and the Five Kings: America's Abdication and the Fate of the World

The Genius of Judaism

Public Enemies: Dueling Writers Take on Each Other and the World (with Michel Houellebecq)

Left in Dark Times: A Stand Against the New Barbarism

American Vertigo: Traveling America in the Footsteps of Tocqueville

War, Evil, and the End of History

Who Killed Daniel Pearl?

Sartre: The Philosopher of the Twentieth Century

Adventures on the Freedom Road: The French Intellectuals in the 20th Century

The Testament of God

Barbarism with a Human Face

CONTENTS

PROLOGUE

I, too, was shocked.

But what shocked me was not only the pandemic.

That sort of disaster has always been with us.

A century ago the Spanish flu killed fifty million people.

Considering only our own era, that which I am old enough to remember, there was the famous "Hong Kong flu" of 1968, from which at least a million earthlings died, their lips blue, from strangulation or pulmonary hemorrhage. In fact, that episode turns out not to be so famous. I looked into it for a column I wrote right at the beginning of the coronavirus pandemic and found that it had been almost completely forgotten.

Ten years before the Hong Kong flu, and no less erased from collective memory and from archives, there had been the "Asian flu," which also started in China before ravaging Iran, Italy, eastern France, and the United States. As many as two million perished, including around a hundred thousand in the United States and probably a like number in France, dying in underequipped hospitals where, the last surviving eyewitnesses recall, cadavers piled up in resuscitation rooms faster than they could be evacuated.

No, the most striking thing is the very strange way we reacted this time around.

It is the epidemic of fear, not only of Covid-19, that has descended upon the world.

We have seen hardy souls suddenly paralyzed.

We have heard thinkers who lived through other wars embracing the rhetoric of the invisible enemy, of frontline and reserve fighters in an all-out public health war.

We have watched Paris empty out, as in Ernst Jünger's journal of the German Occupation during World War II.

We have watched New York and Los Angeles become ghost towns, their avenues as quiet as country lanes, where, as Victor Hugo said, the days were like the nights. We have watched, during these weeks, the Never Trumpers, the Democrats fighting the "America First" trend, the activists for civil rights, women's rights, and human rights go virtual or simply disappear from the radar.

I have observed, in videos sent to me from Kiev, Milan, and Madrid, as well as from Lagos, Erbil, and Qamishli, the passing of the occasional scurrying pedestrian, who seemed to be there only to remind us of the existence of the human species, but who then crossed to the other side of the street, eyes downcast, as soon as another human appeared.

All across the planet, in the most impoverished lands no less than in the great metropolises, we have witnessed entire populations tremble and allow themselves to be driven into their dwellings, or sometimes clubbed in, like game into its burrow.

The demonstrators in Hong Kong have disappeared, as if by magic.

My friends in the Peshmerga, fighters whose name

means "those who go out to meet death," have hunkered down in their trenches.

The Saudis and the Houthis, who had been waging a pitiless, protracted war in Yemen, implemented a brief ceasefire as soon as the first Covid-19 cases appeared.

Hezbollah was staying home.

Hamas, citing eight cases of the virus at the time, declared that their sole military objective was now to obtain respirators from Israel. If necessary, they said, "we'll take them by force."[1] (I can hear Richard III: "A mask! A mask! My kingdom for a mask!")

ISIS declared Europe a risk zone for its fighters, who promptly disappeared to wipe their noses on eucalyptus Kleenex in the depths of some cave in Syria or Iraq, while plotting to stir up trouble in "safer" areas such as Egypt, Yemen, Indonesia, Afghanistan, and the Sahel.

After one suspected Covid-19 case was detected, Panama confined to the jungle 1,700 destitute people who had been trudging north toward the United States.

By mid-April, according to Agence France-Presse, twelve people had died from the virus in Nigeria, whereas eighteen had been killed by security forces for violating the lockdown.[2] Only a few months earlier, I had been reporting on Christian villages wiped out by Fulani jihadists in the north-central part of the country.

Bangladesh, where I had been reporting just hours before France closed its borders, had long been suffering from a multitude of calamities: dengue fever, cholera, plague, rabies, yellow fever, and unknown viruses. But there, too, as soon as a few cases of Covid-19 were reported, the country, acting as one, cinched itself up.

Indeed, the entire planet – rich and poor alike, those with the resources to resist and those without – pounced on the idea of an unprecedented pandemic poised to eradicate the human race.

So . . .

What could have brought this about?

Could it have been viral propagation – not just of the virus itself, but of talk about the virus?

Could it have been collective blindness, as in José Saramago's novel, where a mysterious epidemic robs an entire town of its sight?

Perhaps it was the victory of the collapsologists who, always alert to the end of the world, see it heading toward us once again and are giving us one last chance to repent and reset?

Or the triumph of the masters of the world, who see in this great confinement (the English translation of the *grand renfermement* Michel Foucault spoke of in his early speculations on the power systems of the future in *Madness and Civilization*) a rehearsal of sorts for a new way to arrest, oppress, and detain a mass of people?

Was it a Reign of Terror, akin to the one born after 1789, with its explosion of fake news, conspiracies, frantic flights, and, soon enough, dark uprisings born of hopelessness?

Or perhaps it was the opposite? A reassuring sign that the world had changed, that at last life has been made sacred, that from now on, when we come to a choice between life and economics, life will win out?

Or perhaps it was the opposite of that opposite: a collective panic, aggravated by news channels and social networks that, by reporting to us, day after day, the numbers of those who had died, were still in critical condition, or had recovered, herded us into a parallel universe in which nothing else, anywhere, was news—and, in so doing, drove us quite literally mad. After all, that is how Chinese water torture works – the sound of the drop, repeated endlessly, becomes a fearsome dragon. How would we react if the traffic safety authorities decided to install giant loudspeakers at one-mile intervals to inform us of the day's highway fatalities?

To help me think through this extraordinary global surrender to an event that, though tragic, was in no way unprecedented, I had with me, as I always do, my copy of Étienne de La Boétie's *Discourse on Voluntary Servitude.*

I had my memories of René Girard and his idea of mimetic desire, which is itself a virus and which, like any virus, can trigger a pandemic.

I had in mind Jacques Lacan's idea that, when faced with the emergence of a sharp point of the true "real" (as opposed to the "reality" we have agreed upon), a point that pierces us and against which we pierce ourselves, one that makes a hole in our knowledge but of which we lack even an image (and is that not the case for any new virus?), humanity can choose between denial and delirium, neurosis and psychosis.

Examples of the denial and neurosis are Donald Trump's boneheaded, unspeakably irresponsible attempts to deny the pandemic, his subsequent call to "Liberate Michigan," and the striking tweets in which the lunatic U.S. commander-in-chief promotes conspiracy theories about the birth and propagation of the virus.[3] But wasn't all that a natural fit for someone who has denied science, facts, and truth from the start?

An example of the second choice – psychotic delirium – is the spectacle of leaders so terrified by the threat of a Corona Nuremberg that they deemed it more prudent to put the world on hold, caring little for the outbreaks of hunger, violence against the poor, and authoritarian takeovers that were sure to follow. What prevented us from comprehending the immediate need to remain distant from those we love and to respect the new codes set forth by decent and responsible health workers, while, *at the same time,* understanding that the cost of a new Great Depression would be paid, once again, by the most vulnerable?

Anyway, it was too early to tell which of these explanations might apply.

Even now, as I write, and as we begin to "open up," it is still too soon to crack the code – not only of the virus but of the fear that it has raised.

And because I am still mourning those I have lost, I do not yet have the heart for a fully Brechtian look at the extravagant production that the call to social distancing staged before our astounded eyes.

On the other hand, it *is* time to discuss the effects of all this on our minds and societies.

It *is* time to put our finger on what has begun to take place at the level of what connects us, as well as in the deepest and most obscure parts of ourselves.

And if it is true that "an epidemic is a social phenomenon that has a few medical aspects," as the pioneering nineteenth-century German pathologist Rudolf Virchow liked to say, this is the now-or-never moment to pull ourselves together and try to describe some of the nonmedical aspects of this experience.

Some are positive.

We experienced real moments of civic spirit, solidarity, and mutual assistance.

And we should be eternally grateful to have finally

become aware not only of the existence, but also of the eminent dignity, of an entire population of invisible people (caregivers, cashiers, farmers, freight haulers, garbage collectors, delivery workers) who suddenly became visible.

But other aspects are more troubling.

Appalling words have been said, terrible habits developed, and regrettable reflexes allowed to return.

Principles that I hold dear, principles that represented the best of our Western societies, have been attacked by the virus, and by the virus of the virus, at the same time people were dying.

And because ideas die, too, because they live on the same matter as humans do, and because it is very possible that the pandemic, as it recedes, will leave them on the shore like dead jellyfish, gone without a trace since, like us, they consisted almost entirely of water, it is ideas that I wish to defend here.

The First World Fear (as in the way we refer to the war): midpoint review.

Because time is slipping away, here is my assessment—not a statistical one, but one much more difficult to prepare (isn't that how astonishment works: the ruder the shock, the harder it is to think through?) – of the blows dealt to our innermost metaphysics during this strange crisis. It is not too soon to wage that battle, but the risks and responsibilities of the task no longer fall to the politicians or the physicians.

THE VIRUS IN THE AGE OF MADNESS

CHAPTER 1

COME BACK, MICHEL FOUCAULT— WE NEED YOU!

The first thing that struck me was the rise of "medical power."

The temptation to elevate that power is not new, of course.

There is a long history behind it.

There was Galen, the philosopher-physician who, because he was a physician, was the quasi-spiritual adviser to Marcus Aurelius, Commodus, and Septimius Severus.

There was John Locke, whose student writings at Oxford showed us how much the invention of the rights of man owed to Locke's education in physical well-being.

From the French Revolution on, there has been the figure of the physician-magistrate, exemplified by the philosopher Pierre Jean Georges Cabanis, who escaped the Terror thanks to his medical knowledge.

One understands nothing, Michel Foucault tells us, of the types of discipline meted out by governments in the Classical era if one does not see that they were inspired as much by the hospital model as by the prison model: *Discipline and Punish,* yes, but first *The Birth of the Clinic* and its archaeology of a "medical gaze" that would go on to become the "power/knowledge" of the present day.

Moreover, it is impossible to reread without pinching oneself the pages that Foucault devotes to the management of outbreaks of plague up to the eighteenth century: exile to an island or a ghetto on the outskirts of the city, as was the practice with lepers and the insane, gave way to confinement of entire cities, where all citizens were under house arrest and neighborhood watch patrols wrote up holdouts. Once night fell, everyone was out on their balcony, not to applaud the caregivers but to enable the sanitary authorities to tally up the dead, the dying, and the living.

But until now, never had things gone quite this far.

Was it the growing disdain for public pronouncements?

Was it the last stage of the rejection of elites?

Was it a sign of disoriented authorities who no longer know where to turn? Never had a physician been invited into our households every evening to toll, like a sad Pythius, the number of the day's dead.

Never had we seen, as we did in Europe, heads of state surrounding themselves with scientific councils before daring to speak.

Never had we imagined that, in the United States, the impossible and unhinged Mr. Trump would name an epidemiologist to head a task force, nor that he would consent (in this case, thank God, he did!) to stand behind Dr. Anthony Fauci at the lectern and let himself be contradicted and corrected (at least until he became irritated by the popularity of the man whom the *New Yorker* labeled "America's doctor," by Brad Pitt's impersonations of Dr. Fauci on *Saturday Night Live*, and by the metamorphosis of this adviser into a cult figure interviewed on Snapchat and YouTube by everyone whom Generation Z considers most plugged in).[1]

Never had one seen, on every screen on the planet, the image of commentators yielding the spotlight to hospital spokespersons, newcomers to the forum, sometimes knowledgeable, sometimes less so, but always enveloped in a continuously expanding aura, like Tintin's mysterious star – or a video game in which Dr. Fauci's steely eyes slay the fearsome coronavirus dragon.

I'm not speaking here of the "Coronavirus Cassandras" who had the virtue of having been right before everyone else. I am thinking of Laurie Garrett, Pulitzer Prize–winning author of *The Coming Plague,* whom the *New York Times* labeled the "prophet of this pandemic"; Larry Brilliant, an epidemiologist touted in *Vanity Fair,* who had been warning of a coming pandemic since 2006; Michael Osterholm, another epidemiologist and director of the Center for Infectious Disease Research and Policy at the University of Minnesota; and Bill and Melinda Gates, who flagged this wave of terror well before others.[2]

I have to say that, confronted with a health crisis whose mechanisms remain unknown, we were better off with a white coat than a Yellow Vest, a professional talking head, or, as in the United States, an incompetent, irresponsible, and dangerous president who recommends that citizens treat themselves by ingesting disinfectant and carry arms into state capitols to "liberate" themselves from stay-at-home orders.

Physicians are for the most part admirable people standing on the front line against the pandemic, everyday heroes risking their lives to save ours, superbly brave and dedicated. When one weighs the willfully ignorant and imbecilic cynicism of the American president, who appears to consider one hundred thousand Covid-19 deaths as a vague adjustment variable in a growth trajectory that was supposed to continue at a slowed pace – along a "flattened curve" – until November 2020, it will be said, too, that *any* doctor would be preferable to an irresponsible president. That much is obvious.

But to make physicians into supermen and superwomen and to endow them with extraordinary powers requires a leap that can be taken only with the help of several misconceptions.

First, doctors do not always possess more information than we do, and there is something a little absurd in the blind confidence we place in them. Doctors know, as did French philosopher Gaston Bachelard, that the "scientific truth" we implore them to deliver is never more than a "corrected mistake." They are aware that some among them (not the best or the most reliable, certainly) are no more immune than politicians to hasty judgments (Dr. Oz postulating on Fox News that "schools are an appetizing opportunity" to reopen), chancy forecasts (Dr. Drew proclaiming that "coronavirus is way less serious than influenza" and the probability of dying of the virus is the same as that of "getting hit by an asteroid"), and errors of judgment (Dr. Phil suggesting that "we probably shouldn't have ever started this" – meaning social distancing).[3] They are familiar with the paths that lead nowhere, with endless meanderings. They remember all the viruses whose codes we tried so hard to break before they disappeared on their own without our learning their secret. Since Werner Heisenberg and quantum physics, they have understood that, no offense to Albert Einstein, science's god rolls the dice and upholds uncertainty as her principle. And the inner shiver, the chill, the interior alarm that many of us felt when, glued to our televisions (as earlier generations were glued to the radio) and hearing the by-now-all-too-familiar refrain of "Let's listen to those who know" uttered in the lyrical and reassuring tone used to conceal all abuses of authority, I am sure that the best of the experts felt it, too, and were embarrassed at being forced to pose as something they're not.

Second, we say, "The medical profession this, the scientific community that"; we rhapsodize that researchers around the world are joining hands and singing with one voice.

Except none of this makes any sense. And, being fortunate enough to have arrived at philosophy through the door of epistemology, I know that the "community" of scholars is no more communitarian than any other, that it is riven with fault lines, divergent sensibilities and interests, petty jealousies, esoteric disputes, and, of course, fundamental differences. I know that the research world is a *Kampfplatz*, a battlefield, a free-for-all no less messy than the one Immanuel Kant bemoaned in metaphysics. I know that the schools of thought, with their hypotheses and opinions, make a habit of contradicting each other and that they never win more than a moment's respite, knowing that their adversaries are waving the white flag with one hand while reloading their experimental machine gun with the other. In a word, I know that listening to *the ones who know,* if we are indeed talking about scientists, is tantamount to listening to a nonstop quarrel and, if the listener is a government, to inviting Fireworks and Chaos to sit at the king's table. In any case, "those who know" should be regarded with the same caution that we would exercise in the case of any other professional – that is, not blindly.

By the time these pages are published, where will the world stand with respect to Didier Raoult, the Marseille-based doctor and researcher whose studies asserting the benefits of chloroquine and hydroxychloroquine have provoked heated debates and been repeatedly endorsed (and possibly ingested) by hapless President Trump? No one knows. And, frankly, I couldn't care less. But what interests me are the disputes to which Raoult's personality gave rise. We have witnessed the resentment of some of his peers, the propensity of others still to insist on waiting until testing on mice is complete before ever dreaming of relieving human distress. We have heard the spite of a group that, once the question of the side effects of this old medicine was taken off the table, moved on to critiquing the arrogance, the whimsy, and the looks of Raoult, dubbed the "Gérard Depardieu of science." What did this have to do with the scientific debate? And weren't they forgetting in the process the many great eccentrics who were similarly shot down: in the seventeenth century, William Harvey was dismissed by "anti-circulationists" for his discovery that blood circulates in the body; Thomas Willis, the neurologist who gave us the concept of reflexes using an image of a human body traversed by flames, was considered a crank; in 1793, Joseph Priestley was mocked for having discovered "laughing gas"—that is, the principle of anesthesia; and in the nineteenth century, Charles Darwin was censured at Cambridge for his theory of evolution and Louis Pasteur was attacked by future French prime minister Georges Clemenceau, then a practicing physician, for his theories of vaccination.[4]

All of this has nothing to do, of course, with the asinine debate between science and faith. All doctors have at least this in common: they all take the side of rationalism against the imbecilic obscurantism of those who prefer superstition and magical thinking to reason and thinking. But it is also far from the pure ethos of truth, and far from the uncontestable authority that the same ethos supposedly confers on science. The emperor has no clothes, even if he is a physician. *Especially* if he is a physician. The renowned doctor, the big shot, however formidable and learned he may be, is naked under his white coat. And in that he reconnects with and shares the fate of the rest of humanity.

Third, there is the question of hygienics. Concern for hygiene is a very good thing. American society, like French society, should be grateful for having had, in the nineteenth and twentieth centuries, battalions of physicians and health workers who focused political debate on improving sanitation in working-class neighborhoods, on combating syphilis and alcoholism, and on the rights of all of us to care for ourselves and our bodies.[5] But everyone also knows that there is a *doctrine* of hygienics that goes something like this: health becomes an obsession; all social and political problems are reduced to infections that must be treated; and the will to cure becomes the paradigm of political action. And no one is ignorant of the fact that the effects of that doctrine can be horribly perverse.

One example will suffice. Consider Henri Sellier, who, in 1936, was minister of health in Léon Blum's Popular Front government in France. He was what members of the previous generation would have called a man of good will. Since 1919, he had been the socialist mayor of the Paris suburb of Suresnes, a good mayor who created green spaces, garden cities in the style of Le Corbusier, and, for families of modest means, well-lit, airy housing estates with good recreational facilities. But he surrounded himself with two doctors.

One was Robert-Henri Hazemann, who had formerly served on a town council near Paris. Dr. Hazemann, a communist, was active in the worker's movement and a pioneer of the modern welfare system, including community health centers. He was also obsessed with screening, prevention, fighting bacilli and viruses, mental and family health, and disinfection. He believed that if the principles of Social Darwinism were reversed and made to favor the "least fit," the victims of natural selection, then those principles might have a certain validity. He took very seriously Alexis Carrel's 1935 bestseller, *Man, the Unknown,* which glorified the most shameful eugenics. And this man was the chief technical adviser to Minister Sellier.

The other, Edouard Toulouse, was a physician in Marseille who, in 1921, founded the French Mental Hygiene and Prophylaxis League and preached a bizarre form of Saint-Simonism based on "sanitary renewal" and on preventing procreation by anyone whom the unified, indivisible, and humanistic French Republic could not cure of their "defects." He exhorted others – the "healthy" and those "sanitized" by the green practices of municipal socialism – to multiply at will. More prenuptial medical certificates for them! Because we're counting on them to improve the race! Up with "special allowances for the best human specimens so as to encourage, here as in other areas, a rational selection!"[6]

This is how the special adviser to Léon Blum's health minister spoke. And the minister himself chose similar terms for his lecture in London in June 1936, where, accompanied by his technical adviser, he quoted liberally from Alexis Carrel's book. And so it was quite natural that, in "The Struggle Against Social Evils," an article published around the same time, Henri Sellier wrote that, given the urgency of "defending the race against the certainties of degeneration and destruction revealed in the sorry statistics on births, diseases, and deaths," he favored "a policy of eugenics."[7]

Before dying in 1943, the old militant would have time to see the hygienists of the Vichy government lay claim to his harebrained ideas. He would watch as his projects for planning and improving the collective health of the French people became one of the bulwarks of a regime he abhorred. But his bewildered incomprehension could not change a thing. Ideas are more stubborn than facts. And, in this case, empowering doctors was a Pétainist example of a convenient ruse. Of course, the twenties of our century are not the thirties of the previous one. And, fortunately, we are not at the same point at which hapless Henri Sellier found himself. But we have indeed seen, at the height of the pandemic, our hospital systems retrace, at high speed and in reverse, the steps in the history of the clinic (nosological, epidemiological, anatomical) described by Michel Foucault. Is it too far-fetched, then, to imagine a return, God forbid, to the worst of hygienics?

This is also the right moment to recall one of the first great works of philosophy devoted to the same question, Plato's dialogue the *Statesman.* In it, Plato contemplates passing on to the physician the responsibility for leading the human flock if the divine pastor drops the ball. He lays out the factors that favor such a choice: the structural analogy between the animal body and the civic body; the identical role of the head of the one and the leader of the other; the choice of the same word, *epimeleia,* to designate the care owed to the first and the administration at work in the second. There is just one reason – but a decisive one – why, at the last minute, just as the dialogue is winding up, and with that twinge of truth that always distinguishes philosophical speech from sophistry, Socrates decides otherwise. Politics, he says, is an art that, since the retreat of the gods, deals with a chaotic, changing world, swept by storms and rudderless. But, in a storm, what is the point of a Hippocratic nosology of "cases"? Do not the difficult times call instead for citizen-guardians possessing the audacity and strength to think through, carve into stone, and proclaim legal "codes"?

Cases versus codes. Diagnostics versus laws. On one side of the argument, the physicians who, with their nose in their casework and seeing nothing beyond the organs which, in Paul Valéry's phrase, they have the awesome responsibility of keeping (healthfully) silent, might well have extended the health emergency until hell froze over. On the same side, the chairman of France's science council, announcing to the Senate's disconcerted legislative committee that the academy has "decided" to "delay" the "release from confinement" of "18 million at-risk individuals" who "cannot deal with Covid-19 under reasonable conditions."[8] And also on the same side, an assortment of learned persons to whom some in France would have given full powers, up to and including the power to set the school calendar (would the school year now start in May, as President Emmanuel Macron was proposing, or in September?) and the parameters governing the wealth of the nation (whether to add 10, 20, or 50 percent to the ranks of the unemployed, and never mind the looming recession), even though those learned persons are, once again, specialists in one particular *case*. And alone on the other side, the Platonic recommendation to rely, simply, on the Republic.

In France, the exhortation has been heard. The republican authorities have grasped that, though the physicians are real heroes in one essential arena, they are neither God the Father nor the archons of a city in the grip of a new plague. They have made it known to the sorcerer's apprentices that the silence of the organs must not be the silence of a ceasefire or of a watchtower looming over the bodies of the governed. But that acknowledgment came *in extremis*. After days and days of feverish, asthmatic, harassed agitation during which public opinion clearly wanted to see medicine calling the shots. And only after a sequence of events that very nearly led to the sealing of an incestuous union of the political and medical powers, a union that would have been not only incestuous but fatal for both partners, according to Foucault. What will remain of all that? The imprint, which may or may not endure, of a moment of vacillation? Anything is possible.

CHAPTER 2

DIVINE SURPRISE

There was another thing that I found increasingly difficult to bear as we settled into the crisis.

And that was the rapt remarks I heard, both in conversations among friends and in print, on the theme: "I saw a deer crossing the Champs-Elysées; a hummingbird was at my window; the sky has never been so blue, nor nature so pure, nor New York so beautiful, as during the time of the coronavirus."

I am as sensitive as the next guy to the sweetness of decarbonized air.

I, too, noticed myself experiencing moments of grace at the sight of my city slumbering under the sun, crystalline, abstract.

And it goes without saying (but is just as well said) that I view the fight against climate change as one of the great emergencies of our time and consider climate change deniers (led by Donald Trump and Brazil's Jair Bolsonaro) to be dangerously disingenuous at best and close to criminal.

But, as always, there are good ways and bad ways of putting things.

And there was, in this particular way of admiring nature, an embarrassing combination of pious sentiment, bad instincts, and, for anyone with a modicum of historical sensibility, echoes that were regrettable, to say the least.

First, a Freudian slip and, though it may not seem so at first, a shameful one: the notion that the virus was not altogether bad, that it possessed a hidden virtue, and that there were in this "war" things to be glad about. The shame is obvious. That is how French writer and appeasement advocate Jean Giono sounded in June 1940, just as France was falling to Germany. In the courtyard of the Carrousel du Louvre, Giono enthused about a Paris that had never been so beautiful or in such lush bloom. The same goes for Henry de Montherlant, another pro-Fascist writer. Delivering lectures in Limoges and Lyon in December of the same year, he marveled at the city "without the noise of cars," where "the commotion" was "reined in by the difficulty of transportation." Paul Morand, another writer of the same ilk, sounded a similar note the following year. Having abandoned the French Republic in 1939 to repose in Vichy, by 1941 Morand was charmed by the "disappearance of the billboards," the arrival of "the country air in Paris," and the "renaissance of the horse."[1] But aren't the shame and hypocrisy amply clear to anyone? Who can bear to hear that the overwhelmed hospitals, the tears, the lives cut down have the side benefit of producing a "poetic" or "surreal" New York (I heard both claims)? *Deo gratias . . .*

Next, a sleight of hand that, in the mouths of the most militant, became tantamount to a coup. The litany begins with people's suffering, the cantors perching on the shoulders of the dead and the revived alike. Oozing goodness and contrition, they sing, reminding us that even before the pandemic they warned against the folly of a world that could not continue as it was, a world headed straight into a wall. They fob off on us, disguised as good medicine, old finger-pointing claptrap that they hope this time will stick. With restrained (but cruel) gloating, they hail the revenge of the real, or the natural, over the arrogance of man and his sins. The deviousness of these flagellants, trying their damnedest, from their perch on the backs of the victims, to scold the survivors and overwhelm them with remonstrances! The calls for a change, no less than the streams of reproof and the invitations to rebirth, echo the sermons France heard in 1940, asserting that the country had had too much fun, that it had reaped more than it had sown, that it had marched, said André Gide, "blindfolded, to defeat," and that it was time to turn everything around. But they also echo the words of the proponents of America First in the late 1930s. They, too, viewed the calamities befalling old Europe as the price to be paid for sins that had gone unpunished for too long. In 2020, in any case, both the French and the Americans found themselves in Argos, the city of Aegisthus in Jean-Paul Sartre's *The Flies*, transformed now into a giant penitentiary. Or in Oran, the city of Albert Camus's *The Plague*, with Father Paneloux castigating his flock for their "criminal indifference" and intoning, "Calamity has come to you, my brethren, and, my brethren, you deserved it."[2] We were in La Fontaine, with the king of the animals announcing to his council that Heaven permitted this misfortune because of our sins. *Nostra culpa.*

And, finally, there was a foolish conceit: the idea that the virus is speaking to us, that it has a message to deliver, and that because nothing in this world happens without cause or intention, this particular virus, this *corona*virus, this virus with spikes and a crown, this king of a virus, must be secretly invested, like a cunning ruse of Hegelian history, with a part of the spirit of the world and thus with a mission: to reorchestrate the fanfare of All against the Government; to function as an unsparing critic of failed globalization or, as Ivan Vejvoda said in the *New York Times,* to pose "questions about the interconnectedness of the world as we've built it." According to them, it was the virus that brought into view, as if from invisible ink, the disorders and injustices of the famous "world before" that people were now claiming to have been absolutely detestable. As if a virus could think, know, or intend anything! As if a virus was *living!*

If there is just one thing one should know about a virus, Georges Canguilhem used to tell us, it is that, unlike a microbe, which, etymologically, signifies "small life," a virus is a poison. It is not alive or dead and may be nothing more than the radicalization of, and a metaphor for, Martin Heidegger's concept of "being-toward-death."

If there is one thing to add to Canguilhem's rule, it may be Jacques Lacan's warning that this less-than-nothing, this tiny, furtive monster ready "to spread over the world like the locusts of the Bible," has no name in the Creation, no more so than bacteria, and thus owes part of its existence to scholars – that is, to humans, who, by naming it, pull it from nothingness.[3]

And, finally, you do not have to be Lacan or Canguilhem to understand two things. First, it is an iron law for any progressive that there is never a "good side" to a calamity, never anything positive or useful to be taken from it. And second, there have always been viruses (and bacteria!). Take the Black Plague, which killed nearly half of Europe's population in the fourteenth century. Take the Athens plague reported by Thucydides. The plague of Thebes. The Cough of Perinthus, which furnished the occasion for the Greek language to invent, if not the thing itself, then at least its name, *epi demos,* or, literally, "on the people," and the first calamity that, in contrast to the biblical idea of a "scourge" afflicting the "firstborn," fell on an entire people without distinction as to age, rank, or quality. None of these had anything to do with liberal globalization, the depletion of fossil fuels, or atmospheric concentrations of carbon dioxide. You do not have to be a scholar to notice that, all things considered, viruses were on each of those occasions the weapon nature used in violence against humanity more than a sign of the crime humanity had committed against nature.

From this dark providentialism, this punitive magical thinking, this viral catechism that turned our locked-down dwellings into so many purgatories and lazarettos, no one was exempt.

And perhaps it is a general principle of pandemics: in the face of plague, of the implacable, in the face of the prospect of imminent and indiscriminate death, communities have an irrepressible tendency to bond together in fear and shared repentance and to offer up a promise to the virus god never to return to the old ways but rather to invent themselves anew. This is illustrated, by the way, in *The Horseman on the Roof*, the very great novel of an epidemic – and of freedom amid an epidemic – penned by the same Jean Giono (who was more than just a Pétainist).

But there are two schools of thought that have been particularly egregious, two whose sanctimonious warnings to the effect that the coronavirus is speaking to humanity have done the most damage.

On one end of the spectrum, there are those who believe that human actions "made the virus," arguing that when we disrupt natural habitats and meddle with ecosystems, viruses emerge, or that human overpopulation provokes viral exchanges from animals to humans, as David Quammen argued in the *New York Times*. And there are those who would have us believe that Covid-19 is the direct result of human hubris, interconnectedness, and globalization. Or that "nature is sending us a message," in the words, alas, of Inger Anderson, the executive director of the United Nations Environment Programme. Or, as filmmaker Michael Moore postulated, that the "virus is a gentle warning from the planet before it takes revenge on humanity over climate change."[4]

These ecologists, sovereignists, and antiglobalists wanted us to know that they "knew" all along and saw it all coming. Crying "I told you so," they have been all too happy to remind us that we had to pull back from globalization, manufacture at home, consume fruits only in season, and beware of international markets. "Never Again!" they cried, since one vulgarity more or less won't make a difference.

These imaginary physicians straight out of Molière (no longer insisting "The lung, I tell you!" but now, "The virus, I tell you!") did not want to miss the "rendezvous." (They said that!)

They found the crisis to be "sensational" and "the apocalypse" to be an "exciting" theme.

They were obsessed with the risk of "missing the catastrophe"[5] (they said that, too!) and not being in time to seize the "historic opportunity" offered by the pandemic.

See, in *Politico,* the experts sharing their visions on what the future might bring: "a new kind of patriotism," "a decline in polarization," "a new civic federalism," "a healthier digital lifestyle," "more cooking," and so on.[6]

They plied us day in and day out with their "day after," an evangelical version of the old Leninist Grand Soir, after which nothing would ever be as before because the "ideals of solidarity-equality-moderation" would have "gone viral."[7]

"A warning" from nature, said one, demanding a transition to a world less destructive of biodiversity. "An ultimatum," said another, from a mistreated Gaia whose patience had worn thin. And, from all of them, *servility* with respect to the virus.[8]

The most eminent representative of the servile contingent was French philosopher Bruno Latour, who had the gall to write that the virus is "a tremendous opportunity"; that it is an invisible hand that, with a great "screech of the brakes," will help ecologists advance their "landing program," whatever that means. We are faced with an emergency challenge, he said: to combat the coronavirus spread by becoming, like the virus, "globalization cutoff switches" whose "small, insignificant actions, laid end to end" will do what "the virus does through small exhalations from mouth to mouth"–namely, bring about the revolutionary "suspension" of the "world economy."[9]

This is the old Marxist refrain of the final crisis of capitalism in her morning-after guise of collapsology, or one of the children's diseases of socialism updated as disasterism. I know this all too well, having been born and raised in it! It is disastrous, indeed. And obscene.

At the right end of the right, we have the American Pentecostalists who saw Covid-19 as the judgment of God, a reckoning unleashed on the states that had legalized abortion and marriage for all.

On this side is Ralph Drollinger, the minister who leads a weekly Bible study for Trump's cabinet, assuring us that the virus was God's judgment. Right-wing radio host Rick Wiles claiming that the virus is God's "death angel seeking justice for transgendering children and putting filth on TVs." The French bishop who explained to an empty church that "God uses the troubles that befall us" to encourage us to draw from those troubles "lessons of conversion and purification." A former French government minister who tweeted that "we all knew something was going to happen" and exulted at seeing gentle Mother Earth finally giving us a spanking.[10] And another French politician, Philippe de Villiers, connecting the pandemic with the Notre Dame fire and seeing in it the second warning bell (with the third not far off in his faux-tragic vision of the world) – a drama of punishment that ushers in a new paradigm for a changed world, just as it does for the left.

We have Brazil's Bolsonaro, proposing a national fast to exorcise the demon and implore him to take pity.

We have a radical Islamic preacher, Hani Ramadan, brother of Brother Tariq, for whom the virus was the fruit of our "turpitudes" and could, if we wished (and if its victims were celebrated as martyrs) be turned into a call for a return to Sharia law.[11]

Not to mention Turkey's Recep Tayyip Erdoğan, ordering everyone under twenty and over sixty-five to stay home. And Chechnya's Ramzan Kadyrov, taking advantage of the quarantine to identify and eliminate some of his opponents. And, in Europe, Hungary's Viktor Orbán eagerly reading the nanometric tea leaves of the modern coronavirus to justify new moves in his illiberal takeover, as if these had not been waiting in the wings.

This boils down to more Father Paneloux (from Camus's *The Plague*), ending his sermon on the victims of Oran's epidemic with a peroration on the virtues of suffering: "This same pestilence which is slaying you works for your good and points your path."[12] It amounts to more Aegisthus (from Sartre's *The Flies*) exhorting the new Thebes to beat its breast and "follow the path of redemption."

A moment later, these profiteers of the virus, buoyed by the wind of conspiricism blowing across the planet, were off on a hunt, not for patient zero but for guilty party zero and, as in La Fontaine's fable, the accursed, mangy animal (some would say the scapegoat) whose excesses brought "celestial wrath" down upon us and whose sacrifice was necessary to lift the plague. The only thing missing was the man with his forehead smudged with ashes, the wandering Jew, walking, in Eugène Sue's telling, at the pace of "brother Cholera." And we got there soon enough. Among far-right agitators, the indictment of the "Chinese virus" was quickly followed by the announcement of a "Judeo-virus," worse than the coronavirus. This led, in turn, to a variety of wild claims. The virus was designed by Israel as a biological weapon, according to Paul Nehlen, white supremacist and failed congressional candidate. From the

Nation of Islam's "research group," we heard that Israel had developed the virus for political assassinations. A Swiss Holocaust denier claimed that George Soros was spreading the virus through his biological laboratories in Wuhan.[13]

Confronted with so much opportunism, with an interpretive fever in which all parties seemed to want to think of themselves as the exclusive augury of the world after the virus (whereas they were doing no more than setting a date with themselves), I began to miss the lessons in simplicity offered by Dr. Rieux in *The Plague* and Orestes in *The Flies*.

And, like them, like the two enemy brothers united, like a cool Jean-Paul Sartre reconciled with an appeased Albert Camus, the two joining in the same struggle against the Furies who roam the city of the dead, I was surprised that more of us were not rising up to oppose the glut of cynicism with two simple principles that are, in a pandemic, the beginning of wisdom.

The first was political.

More than most, I am a partisan of repairing the world.

More often than I should, I cite Walter Benjamin's

phrase about the need to activate History's emergency brake.

And I, too, dream of seeing the ecological principle become a permanent part of our legal codes.

But not like this. Not all of a sudden. Not through this catastrophic, even apocalyptic interruption, with its incalculable consequences.

Because calculation, in fact, is what was (and is) needed.

To the extent possible, we had to calculate the number of lives saved by shutting down the world and compare it with the number imperiled by the shutdown.

We had to be reminded that the social, economic, and health consequences of the shutdown "will be long lasting and calamitous, possibly graver than the direct toll of the virus itself," in the words of David L. Katz, founding director of the Yale-Griffin Prevention Research Center. In an op-ed entitled "Is Our Fight Against Coronavirus Worse Than the Disease?," Katz suggested that a targeted approach would be better than a "horizontal interdiction" in which we close up shop across the board, regardless of the social, humanitarian, and economic cost.[14]

A more sensitive approach would weigh the risks, in the most fragile countries, and, at home, in the most vulnerable populations, of dying of the disease against those of perishing from a preexisting pathology aggravated by the lockdown. One of those pathologies is hunger, which each day kills twenty-five thousand men, women, and children around the world.

In other words, it was important not to be intimidated by the ultimately false opposition between "life" and "the economy," but to compare the cost, in lives, of the spread of the virus with the cost of the self-induced coma triggered in a planet that was transformed suddenly into a laboratory for a radical political experiment.

The only way of making that comparison was to launch a major democratic debate and to go into detail, not about our diverting utopias concerning the *world after,* but about the concrete measures to be implemented here and now in the *world during.*

The governments of the world did not take that course, you say?

They decided to place their countries in blackout mode and simply declare a global health emergency?

True.

But that was no reason to fall slavishly into step with the official course.

Yet this was the first time we had ever seen all of the critical minds in the far-left galaxy applaud a state of emergency.

But not all of the larger group of critical minds. Writing two days after Katz, the wise Thomas Friedman, in his weekly column in the *New York Times,* warned that we could "kill many people by other means, kill our economy and nearly kill our future." And as I write these words, the editorial board of the *Wall Street Journal* has echoed what I have been urging in my columns in Europe for some time: that the choice between lives and jobs is incorrect. As they put it, "much of the media continue to treat the economic destruction as a sideshow and present a false choice between saving lives and jobs. But this is the fastest jobs collapse in modern history. The Great Depression drove millions of Americans into poverty and caused many suicides, and there's a substantial risk this could happen again."[15]

To my mind, a thinker, even a radical one, could

fulfill his function better by saying, "Look, governments, amid storm and stress, you have put your economies on simmer; and perhaps there was no better choice at the outset; but that decision presents, for the lives one is seeking to save, dangers that no one has been able to measure. Now we want to see the media devote even a fraction of the time it squanders on inconclusive discussions among 'adult toddlers' in 'starched lab coats' who are 'playing with things unknown'[16] to debates between economists, demographers, geopolitical analysts, elected officials, and ordinary citizens exploring these dangers, clarifying the present, and, instead of idiotic hackathons and other phony consultations in which commentators speculate on daily life in the world after, examining concretely, precisely, and in detail the complexity of the measures that need to be taken, *in the world now,* to combine the health emergency with the protection of people's livelihoods."

The other principle was metaphysical.

All my life I have fought against the trap of secular religiosity.

Since my early days, when I wrote *Barbarism with a Human Face* and first read Lacan, I have maintained that assigning a sense or meaning to something that has none and putting words to the beyond-sense that is the inexpressible fact of human suffering is one of the sources of psychosis at best, and totalitarianism at worst.

And I have always thought that it does no one any good to reduce politics to the clinic, to classify as "disorders" the parts of man that are death and evil, or to claim to be able to cure the human race of those conditions.

So it seems to me appropriate, confronted with obscurantism with a scientific face, to recall two things.

I will repeat, first, that viruses are dumb; they are blind; they are not here to tell us their stories or to relay the stories of humanity's bad shepherds; and consequently there is no "good use," no "societal lesson," no "last judgment" to be expected from a pandemic, nothing to be drawn from it except simple, unemotional observations on the state of a health system (for example) and the fact that we never spend enough, anywhere, for research teams or hospitals.

And next, as Canguilhem taught us, the questions of immunity, recovery, and biological innocence, the relations between the normal and the pathological, health and illness, and life and death, are, epistemologically, much murkier than we have been led to believe over the past few months.

What is a virus? Is it a thing in itself, an essence visiting the body of the patient, something that one can separate from the body and treat in isolation? Or is it instead, as post-Bachelardian epistemology established, a dysfunction in the collection of organs and pathologies that makes a given subject unique? If it is the second, the directors of the blockbuster War Against the Virus, the new Dr. Purgons promising that they were on the way not only to containing it but to purging society of it and eradicating it, should think again.

What is a body? Is it made up of silence and confinement? Or rather, is it – as taught by true medicine, the medicine that grew from the classification systems of the ancients to the clinical-anatomical method described by Foucault and Canguilhem – a set of miasms, mucuses, coughs, sputums, fears, pathologies, terrors, sweat-drenched nightmares, and bodies attached to other bodies – all capped by the freedom that hovers over all disorders and that Nietzsche called "the great health"?

In which case the Purgons are Diafoiruses who dare not confront the evidence that humanity has always lived, and will continue to live, with its viruses.

To them all, to the rentiers of drama and death, to the bio-dolatrous ventriloquists who made Covid-19 speak (as old-time radio used to give voice to Edgar Bergen's Charlie McCarthy and Mortimer Snerd), to the thaumaturgists who adored their beautiful virus as Dante did Beatrice and whose armchair catechism could not conceal how little importance they attached to real people and their pain, to the invasive chatterboxes whose positivistic religiosity drowned out the voices of the care-givers on too many days, I was dying to say, "Shut up! Please just shut up."

One day or another, the virus will be tamed.

By then, will we have forgotten their screeching? I hope so.

CHAPTER 3

DELICIOUS CONFINEMENT

But there is another phrase that I have come to find unbearable.

It is the quotation from Blaise Pascal, spouted ad nauseam: "All of man's misfortune comes from one thing, which is not knowing how to sit quietly in a room."

And the way the quotation became a sacrament for another population of penitents, or the same one, when they discovered they had made yet another mistake. Ravaging the planet, sure. Permitting the globalization of supply chains for food and health care, check. Taking frequent plane trips (each a blow to the carbon balance and a crime against the climate), yes, certainly. But in doing these things, in projecting themselves outwardly toward the world, they had been turning away from themselves, from their inner truth, and from the long view to which they aspired – which staying at home would fortuitously remedy.

But the quotation from Pascal was truncated.

Confinement's happy few, the lucky ones who went off to tend the garden of their country house, and all the other joyful and good-humored confinees who had the good fortune not to be living in a nursing home, a high-rise block in East Harlem or the Bronx, or a one-bedroom apartment with noise and children, all the neo-urbanites who saw in Pascal's thought an invitation to rediscover the simple pleasures, the delights of time standing still, the joy of daily rituals relearned, but above all the chance to find their center again and listen to themselves living, did not know how to read a sentence all the way to the end. They ignored two things. First, for Pascal, "sitting quietly in a room" was not an indulgence but a struggle, a test, an almost intolerably painful metaphysical experience, one that confronts us with our finiteness. Second, that test consisted of doing nothing, strictly nothing, and certainly not cooking, gardening, crocheting, yoga, attending Zoom happy hours, flower pressing, scrapbooking, indulging in home spa treatments, dying fabrics using turmeric powder, making papier-mâché models of Notre Dame, or taking pictures of oneself doing nothing and posting them to the same Instagram account where the week before one had posted vacation photos. They had simply forgotten that, for Pascal, the test was a test not only of nothingness, but of the vertigo and terror it induced.

Worst of all, these Sunday Pascalians, or six-Sunday Pascalians, these once dead and now resuscitated souls; these formerly errant strivers who, having seen in confinement a chance to calm down, to reboot and replenish, and to reconnect, in Paul Valéry's phrase, with "harmonious Me," would never go back to living like spinning tops (swear to God!); these repenters of entertainment marveling at an old bathrobe and slippers that they'll never change out of because those comfy old things will help them in the uplifting quest to finally become their true selves, focused squarely on themselves and on what is good and precious within them – well, they were all forgetting another of Pascal's maxims, which is the correlate of the previous one: "The self is hateful."

Yes, indeed!

That confinement should have been necessary for public health reasons is one thing.

As a civic obligation, and out of respect for overloaded and overexposed caregivers, I, too, spent these weeks observing the rules.

But to bask in confinement, to settle into it, not to notice its foul odor, to forget that in Italy, for example, the word is redolent of the exiling of anti-Fascists such as Antonio Gramsci (confined to Ustica) or Carlo Levi (Lucania), to find virtue in the thing, to congratulate oneself for the new adventure and the relationship to the world that it established, to start every conversation by indulging in an exchange about confinement status or what television series to binge-watch next, and never to hang up without bidding the other "best wishes for lockdown," as if the couch were the trenches, accepting as self-evident the twisted invitation to gear up to slow down, to stand together and apart, to move closer to one another while staying at home, all under the pretext that it would allow us to get back to essentials (that is, to the reexamination, relearning, and reappreciation of one's self) – that was, for at least two reasons, indecent in the extreme.

It was an insult to those who did not have a home to stay in; it was an offense to the homeless in Chinatown (where Meals on Wheels had their hands full); it was an affront to those who had nowhere to sleep after the New York subway closed for nightly cleaning, to the undocumented in Las Vegas or Los Angeles, and to migrants in general; and it was a snub to the poorest of the poor, who, though they may have had a home in, say, Rio's favelas to Johannesburg's townships, it was so precarious that the occupants dreamed only of getting out.

And the putative wisdom supposedly recovered! The invitation to a journey within four walls accompanied by a philharmonic of trivialities, minor pleasures, and drumrolls of well-tempered narcissism. The idea that confinement is the now-or-never opportunity to do one's internal housekeeping and rediscover the self-to-self relationship that is supposedly the richest of all human relationships. All of that was the exact opposite of what is most honorable in man's vocation.

It flew in the face of Greek wisdom, which, from Aristotle on, held that man was a political animal.

It contradicted René Descartes, who knew that the experience of doubt, of the hearth, of being cooped up in the cogito, is, as it was for Pascal, a discrete moment of consciousness, only a moment, before consciousness rediscovers its zest for the sciences, for medicine, for ethics (both provisional and absolute), for intellectual speculation, for friendship, and for the world.

It went against Edmund Husserl's phenomenology, which, in opposition to all forms of subjective essentialism, comes down to the idea that consciousness is always *conscious of something,* that existence is rooted in intentionality, and that what is interesting about a given subject is not what he is but what he does and, in doing what he does, how he inhabits the world, shapes it, takes from it, and gives to it.

These smug masters of the art of confinement, confiding on their blogs that they had never been so happy or so free since finding themselves right where they were, with nothing to occupy them, nearly motionless in their rooms, suspended in the current of time, had, I found, an irritating tendency to sound like Mr. Simonnot in Sartre's *The Words*. Mr. Simonnot was so happy to be right where he was, so happy to be in the place that was his own, fortified as if it were the most precious of assets, that whenever for some reason he was not at home, whenever he found himself somewhere else, he imagined his colleagues exclaiming, "Whoa! Mr. Simonnot is missing from his spot!" For Sartre, the great phenomenologist and Pascalian standing before the eternal, Mr. Simonnot was the embodiment of a deplorable person. Equating everything to the self, feeling certain that I am confined to me, and enveloping the self in self-satisfaction and self-congratulation – that, for Sartre, was the very definition of the deplorable.

Not to mention Emmanuel Levinas, who was convinced that the affirmation and enjoyment of the ego, far from being the path to a paradise of wisdom, is, for any subject, a formula for poison. Humanity, for Levinas, begins with an injunction that is exactly the opposite: others first. The ego, fine, but only on the condition that it moves immediately toward others, meets them, allows itself to be taken in, filled, and even exhausted by their otherness. The self, yes, if you insist, provided that it otherizes and expatriates itself, spills over from its confines and makes itself the host, the hostage, the possession of its neighbor. An ethic not of interiority but of *faces,* that is, of responsibility and of the infinite unmasked. All the rest, said the author of *Difficult Freedom,* is lies, injustice, and violence inflicted on meaning.

I complied, of course, with the practices and actions recommended to slow the spread, known in French as *gestes barrières,* literally "blocking actions."

But, in this very word, in the social distancing urged upon us, in the safety zones that we were exhorted to erect around ourselves, and in the wearing of masks (which is changing the look of our cities as the virus spreads), was there not something radically opposed to Levinas's ethic of faces and of ethics in general?

And what about the reflex of no longer shaking hands, which seemed to take hold without too much regret? Shaking hands was a fine gesture of civility. It was a sign of republican solidarity promoted by the American Revolution, the spirit of democracy, the Quakers, and so on. If the new practice were to endure, if people decided they liked it, if the exception became the rule in an era when mutual distrust needed no help in spreading, if Anthony Fauci proved to be right when he told the *Wall Street Journal,* "I don't think we ever should have to shake hands again, to be honest with you," would we not lose something dear and cherished?[1]

During those weeks, I had several conversations with Jewish thinkers.

Confinement, they argued, is found in the Torah, is it not? Were not Egypt's Jews ordered to stay in their homes while the angel of death took the firstborn of Egyptian families? Did Moses not confine Aaron and his sons in a tent for seven days while awaiting the sign of an unprecedented revelation? Did not Rabbi Nachman of Breslov recommend *hitbodedut,* or withdrawal into oneself? And what about Hillel's famous dictum (which, like Pascal's, has been beaten to death)? Did Hillel not ask, "If I am not for myself, who will be for me?"

I understood, of course.

I listened respectfully to the rabbis and hospital chaplains.

But I remembered my old friend Benny Lévy, the

French Maoist leader and personal secretary to Sartre who turned to the study of the Torah, inviting me to ponder the rest of Hillel's saying. Yes, of course, "If I am not for myself, who will be for me?" But Hillel followed that immediately by asking, "If I am only for myself, what am I?"[2] Notice that Hillel said "what," not "who." He wanted us to understand clearly that if I am "only for me," I become a "what," a neutral being without qualities, a half-being, a thing. If I graze in the meadow of this me, he insisted, if I confine myself within the me-substance and the persevering ego (a specialty of the West that Covid-19 has raised to the Pantheon), then I am not much of anything; I am a subject without a predicate, a thing without qualification. I place myself under the tyranny of the object. Did someone say "the cult of me"?

I thought of Rabbi Nachman's tomb in Uman, Ukraine. It happens I was there a few years ago and saw a crowd of pilgrims very much unconfined, a joyous, jostling, holy bustle. And I remembered a remark from one of them, a Frenchman, who was amused by my surprise: "*Hitbodedut,* retreat, withdrawal into yourself—that's an experience that counts, for sure, but it's only one experience; it's a radical experience with a limit; and at the limit of that experience, on its horizon, lies the splendor of the world, not the poverty of the ego reflected in a mirror and wallowing in its confinement." Will the pilgrimage take place this year? Would the individual with whom I spoke express himself in the same terms today, during the time of the coronavirus? And if he did, would he be charged with a crime? Probably. And yet . . .

I thought back on my delighted discovery of the prophets forty years ago, when I was writing *Le testament de Dieu.* Prophecy is inherently an act of exposure to another intelligence, and even a radically different one, since it is God's. From the first day of the flight from Egypt to the last word of Obadiah, Joel, and Malachi, the act of prophecy involves stepping outside the self and off one's home ground. And when one takes refuge in the "camp," is it to teach Israel the virtues of confinement or to remind it of a unique test, one that the Hebrews experienced on the eve of leaving Egypt? The test came at the moment when, while contemplating the blood of the paschal lamb on the doors of their houses, they had the strange sensation of being simultaneously on Pharaoh's land and no longer being on it, of being slaves of the self yet already on the path toward the Endless, filled with the feeling of crossing nothingness.

The more I thought about it, the more it seemed that I could approach the matter from any angle, and even from the two extremes of the Jewish experience, which are supposedly mutually exclusive. A liberal, universalist, humanist Jew – one for whom a "perspective" is valid only if it resolves into an "ethic" and puts that ethic in the driver's seat – can experience confinement within oneself only as a regrettable temporary state, one that, if it were to endure, would be starkly contrary to his vocation, which is to move toward his fellow men. The other, the studious Jew, is told to acquire a master, because there is no shaping of the self without a searing exposure to one who knows more than you, but also to acquire a companion, for study is done in pairs, as philosophy was for Plato. That Jew experiences the *pilpul* as hand-to-hand combat between two people, full of collisions and clashes etched into their physical and spiritual selves, replaying over and over the *milhamta shel Torah*, the war of Torah, which is the only true way to take on the Torah.

Over those weeks we saw popping up in the media writers' "journals of confinement."

And, to build our trust in their auto-fictional exercises, we could rely on the list of the greats who had produced masterpieces from sequestration: Franz Kafka ("The Burrow"), Xavier de Maistre (*Voyage Around My Room*), Jean Genet in prison, Friedrich Hölderlin in his tower, Marcel Proust in his cork-lined room, Roland Barthes in the sanatorium, Michel de Montaigne in his library, Henry David Thoreau in a cabin on Walden Pond, Emily Dickinson at Amherst, Elizabeth Barrett Browning, Thomas Mann (the essential *Magic Mountain*), René Crevel in Davos, Thomas Bernhard in quarantine (volume four of *Gathering Evidence*), Oscar Wilde (*De Profundis*), Marquis de Sade, François Villon, Fyodor Dostoevsky, Edward Bunker (*Stark*), Dino Buzzati (*Tartar Steppe*), Ezra Pound – the list goes on and on.

But apart from the fact that it was difficult to detect any sign of a talent remotely comparable to those masterpieces in the descriptions inflicted on us of blooming camellias, of seagulls returning to the Île Saint-Louis, of winter dawns and early springs; in the brave metaphors comparing the suffocation of the dying to that of the exhausted planet; or in the recounted words of children being subjected to repeated viewings of Roberto Benigni's *Life Is Beautiful* and asking, "Is the planet tired, like mama?" – apart from that, there remained a major difference between the confinees of yesterday and today's.

Among those that the latter-day chroniclers of confinement have allowed themselves to cite as precedents, there were invalids (Proust), madmen (Hölderlin shut up for thirty years in a tower in Tübingen), and prisoners (Sade, de Maistre, Pound, Dostoevsky, Villon). Except perhaps for de Maistre, I do not believe that any of them fell into the trap of seeing their trip to the dungeon as a lucky opportunity to be seized.

Genet was even clearer, writing *Our Lady of the Flowers* out of hatred for his forced confinement and for the "exaggerated judgments" passed by frivolous and ignorant officials. In *Miracle of the Rose,* he describes a prison "shorn of its sacramental ornaments," reduced to its cruel nakedness, where "the inmates are merely sorry creatures with teeth rotted by scurvy," shuffling along "on canvas slippers which are eaten away and stiff with filth that the dust has compounded with sweat."[3]

And last I will cite a text by René Crevel, the other great suicide of surrealism, written after reading an article by Emmanuel Berl on "sanatorium literature" and the presumed good use that a whole generation of writers, according to the bourgeois author of a work about the death of bourgeois thought, were going to be able to make of their illness. "Mr. Berl is a pamphleteer and necrophile," the young Crevel wrote in the first issue of *Le Surréalisme au service de la révolution.* Mr. Berl makes "hollow cheeks and pinched nostrils" into the "morbid stigmata" of genius. Mr. Berl is a would-be Prometheus, "mistaking for an eagle the pains in his liver." Mr. Berl confuses the "awful care factories in which I suffer and suffocate" with a school of "style and inspiration." Mr. Berl, "astounded by his own Berlisms," is an ass to whom "I say, in eight very lucid letters, bullshit."[4]

The same story.

Neither Crevel nor Genet was a master of the art of confinement.

Their writings were acts of revolt against the swamp,

the moist gastric intimacy, the enzymatic digestion of the self that Sartre held confinement in the self to be.

They knew that Pascal's room, Thoreau's hut, and especially their own den was a dark chamber, an unhealthy space full of resentment; they knew that one is nothing when alone, that one thinks most often of nothing at all, and that hell is not other people, but the self.

CHAPTER 4

LIFE, THEY SAY

But my mind returns to the caregivers.

The other night, like everyone else, I found myself hypnotized by the nonstop images of admirable men and women battling disease and saving lives. What came back to me at that moment was a strange saying from the Talmud that I heard long ago from the lips of Emmanuel Levinas on one of the last visits I paid to him: "The best of doctors are destined for hell."

I found the original text.

It is in the *Mishnah Kiddushin* 82a.

Rabbi Yehuda is speaking in the name of Abba Gurya.

And at the end of a dizzyingly subtle dialogue

rich in paradoxes resolved and with humor, as so often in the Talmud, the rabbi says, "the best of doctors, to Geihinom."

What could that mean?

How could a master of the Talmud say such a strange, shocking thing?

Was it irony?

Provocation?

When one grasps how many great physicians the Jewish people have given to humanity (thanks particularly to Judaism's quintessential emphasis on study); when one remembers that Maimonides was the court physician to the sultan of Egypt, and that Ovadia Sforno, the rabbi of the Italian Renaissance known for his commentaries on the books of Jonas, Job, and Ecclesiastes, was a physician in Rome; when one realizes that Alexander Borgia and Julius II entrusted their papal and royal bodies to none other than Rabbi Samuel Sarfati; when one thinks back on Francis I of France, the prisoner of Holy Roman Emperor Charles V, wasted by syphilis, nearing death, and demanding a Jewish physician (and then another, because the first was a Marrano) – how can we, equipped as we are with our modern ears, possibly understand such a counterintuitive, nearly unintelligible, and scandalous phrase?

I looked in Rashi: every physician, he says, commits errors and abuses his power. That he should be the "best" makes these offenses even more inexcusable. So, to hell you go.

In Meiri, the thirteenth-century Catalan rabbi and enlightened friend of the sciences: the best sometimes operate without being sure that the intervention is necessary. In so doing, they abuse their knowledge. So, again, to hell they go.

In Maimonides, the consummate Talmudist: the same doctor, using the same treatment, can kill one patient and cure another. Another reason he should go to hell.

I happened on this commentary by Jacob Ben Asher, a fourteenth-century legal scholar and pillar of rabbinic wisdom: He who goes to hell is the one who was made to be the best doctor in the world but who shirked his mission in favor of another career. Hell, once again.

But it was in the Maharal of Prague that I found

the most thorough and ultimately the most edifying clarification of this bizarre phrase: (1) the best doctor is the one who, with unbounded passion, gives himself over to the body's examination, hygiene, and cure; (2) that body, the body alone, the body organic, the body, healthy or ill, formed, lest we forget, by a bolt of lightning from the spirit, is nothing more than a bundle of opaque and saturnine matter; and (3) that opaque matter, that body without light or soul, that flesh when treated as if it were unbound from human intelligence and its projects and plans, that body reduced to a mass of organs, humors, and nerves – that is hell in a nutshell. Hell, for the Maharal of Prague, is not the self, as it is for Blaise Pascal. It is not other people, as for Jean-Paul Sartre. It is not the dark room of Jean Genet, Fyodor Dostoevsky, Edward Bunker, and others. Hell is the body. Solely the body, and the body alone. Hell is you, it is me, it is us – but because we are trapped in our bodies, reduced to our bodily life, and, under the sway of medical power – or simply power claiming medical power, or our own subjection to both – we consent.

At that point, things were getting clearer:

The discomfort that had filled me from the first moment, concerning our incredible docility in the face of the encroaching health regimen and the peremptory notice issued to our bodies.

My surprise when I learned that people were hoarding basic necessities, particularly food products with which to feed the body as one might cram a goose.

The fact that few seemed shocked, at least in France, that books were not considered basic necessities. Nourishment for the mind and the soul. A lot of brave bookstores took note. Local click-and-collect initiatives emerged allowing those of us who could not live without books to pick up orders on the sidewalk outside the store. We even saw a former physician who had become a book dealer express amazement that Amazon and other online retailers considered as "essential goods" the categories of high tech and office computing, nutrition, food and beverages, health and body care, and "everything for animals," but not books – and set about to cover Paris on a motor scooter doing deliveries. But those initiatives were ignored, mocked, or condemned on social networks for violating the emergency regulations.

The walking of pets, which was added on April 11 to the list of allowable exceptions to the stay-at-home order in France, whereas solitary and couples' walks on streets and beaches continued to be prohibited.

The closing or suspension of activity at churches and synagogues, bastions of civilization, and at museums, parks, and other sites of lay meditation in which humanity satisfies its uncountable, noncommercializable spiritual needs.

The sight of a sovereign Pope, heir to John Paul II's "Be not afraid" and a veteran practitioner of the eminently Catholic ritual of the blessing of the sick and afflicted in the slums of Buenos Aires, distancing himself from the flock, communicating only through the internet, ordering that fonts of holy water be emptied, and performing the stations of the cross in the courtyard of the basilica facing an empty St. Peter's Square.

Erased, the Jewish image of the Messiah waiting among the scrofulous beggars outside the gates of Rome.

Forgotten, Jesus's healing of the leper, which inspired so many beautiful pages by Gustave Flaubert, François Mauriac, and others.

Out of mind, Violaine, the "pure young girl" of Paul Claudel's *Annonce faite à Marie (The Annunciation of Marie)*. If he were to write the play today and dared to sanctify the luminous young heroine who kisses a leper, contracts leprosy herself, loses her fiancé, confines herself to a cave, and, through faith, revives her fiancé's child, Claudel would be labeled an irresponsible, antisocial citizen with no respect for his neighbors.

Unthinkable, the disturbingly beautiful image I have retained from childhood of General de Gaulle visiting Tahiti two years before his return to power in 1958. His limousine is blocked by a procession of lepers. He gets out, shakes their hands, holds a child in his arms, hugs the organizer of the strange demonstration, says nothing, and continues on his way.

Burials, reduced at the peak of the pandemic to their simplest form. Nearly forgotten, the beautiful phrase about ashes to ashes, dust to dust, and unto dust thou shalt return. Whisked away, the moment of the coffin being lowered into the ground, without which many of us cannot really say goodbye to a loved one.

Death itself. The right to die and to live one's own

death. That moment for each of us, as Michel Foucault said, the most private and secret of our entire existence, the very last instant, the limit, when power no longer has any hold over us and when we call out (as Foucault did, with his last breath, "Call Canguilhem, he knows how to die!") for the one who will help us cross over. All of that, all that knowledge, that immemorial and decisive scene, yanked away for a period of weeks in a gesture of prophylactic impatience that you never thought could happen that way – bodies wrapped in white plastic, like letters dumped in a mailbox; corpses found decomposing in trucks outside a funeral home in Brooklyn, where the director said "bodies are coming out of our ears"; cursory funerals; goodbyes on WhatsApp.[1]

Seniors abandoned in their nursing homes, another sign of savagery. Already there were weaknesses in nursing homes and reports of terrible neglect. But the virus exacerbated those weaknesses and brought the worst to the fore. In New Jersey, corpses were piled up in a shed next to a nursing home. In Greater Houston, more than eighty residents and staff tested positive in a single home. All around the country, basic sanitary protocols were not observed, making the homes a recipe for catastrophe or, as New York governor Andrew Cuomo said, a "feeding frenzy." And now, as this book goes to press, some fifty thousand people have died in nursing homes, accounting for at least 40 percent of all Covid-19 deaths in the United States.[2]

The fight over beds in the hospitals. It is a fight that most have managed to stay out of. But what are we to make of the department head at Saint-Antoine Hospital in Paris stating calmly that "for the very old," going through "ventilation and intubation" will be "more harmful" than "coordinated care and support"? Or of the American bioethicists like Larry R. Churchill, who, at an open forum hosted by the Hastings Center, urged the oldest patients not to overburden resuscitation facilities, to allow the youngest to be tested and vaccinated first, to kick the bucket quietly, at home, or, as in Japanese folklore, on a mountaintop?[3]

And what about all those digital applications that just yesterday we distrusted, often seeing them as enemies of humankind? Think again! Now they have become the platforms for healthy, hygienic, dietetic, and contact-free commerce. Clean! The Big 4 tech giants – Google, Apple, Facebook, and Amazon – criticized as plagues prior to the current plague, were transformed into benign purveyors of tele-work, tele-teaching, tele-consultation, tele-transport, tele-exercise, tele-health, and tele-surveillance, to the point where the World Health Organization joined forces with the video game industry as part of the Play Apart Together campaign, which essentially encouraged children to play video games as a means of social distancing.[4]

And finally, the absence of deep debate over the digital tracing proposals that have been presented throughout the West as the surest way to open up safely.

An infringement of liberty? Delivering into the hands of corporations, not to mention governments, a trove of data that everyone knows can be put to bad uses? More frightening still will be this: living in a perpetual state of alert and suspicion, monitoring our Bluetooth devices, tracking our suspicious contacts, frantically demanding the name – yes, name, you don't kid around with health! – of the stranger you passed this morning, the one with the shady look, the face that was not quite right, and who the app tells us may have infected us.

From the stranger on the street to the colleague in the office, no one will be immune to scrutiny. The security company that uses biometrics to verify people's identities has launched a new product, Health Pass by CLEAR, that will help employers screen their employees. Restaurant groups, airlines, and major retailers are all looking to new programs to collect health data on their workers in order to decide who returns to work and who stays home.[5]

Of course, some strong-minded individuals and institutions have voiced their concerns. The American Civil Liberties Union, for example, has warned of the dangers and published "Principles for Technology-Assisted Contact Tracing." Four Republican senators introduced the Covid-19 Consumer Data Protection Act. Democratic senators countered with the Public Health Emergency Privacy Act, intended to ensure that collected data are not abused. A report from the Brookings Institution stated that contact-tracing apps were not the solution. A strongly worded op-ed in the *Wall Street Journal* by Federal Trade Commissioner Christine Wilson warned against infringements of the Fourth Amendment.

Of course, many Americans are not comfortable

subscribing to the tracing applications. Skeptics cite the example of antiterrorist policies to remind us that it is always easier to suspend a freedom than to restore it. In that vein, Americans remember the Patriot Act of 2001, which curtailed liberties in return for a "new world." Said retired General Stanley McChrystal: "You have this emotional, do-something response, as we saw with 9/11." Alan Rozenshtein, a lawyer in the national security division of the Justice Department in the Obama administration, detected "the same inflection point" as in the U.S. response to 9/11. And, while all the data-mining firms, like Palantir Technologies, which helped unearth Osama bin Laden, now have contracts with the Centers for Disease Control and Prevention, many Americans object to being "traced" for the sake of public health and wonder where they should draw the line.[6]

And, again, there have been some useful media investigations in France into the return to old-style tattling, as measured by the epidemic of "tips" reported to the police, with hotlines submerged by callers, some anonymous, some not, reporting that they had seen an old man going into the supermarket twice in close succession, a woman coming in to buy just one roll of toilet paper, a Parisian man who was turning up every night, or a suspicious assembly of more than two people. The same phenomenon appears to be at work in the United States. Seventeen thousand calls that flooded the police hotline in New York City were nonstarters or dead ends.[7]

But the truth is that the only debate that has truly engaged Europe and the United States is the one about the comparative vices and virtues of the Korean and Chinese, Thai or Singaporean, Confucian or liberal models for compelling people to meet health requirements. To their credit, a number of so-called learned persons have wondered out loud, perhaps while in the grip of a scrap of Marxist memory, whether, having arrived at this point, and, as was already the case in Poland, wanting to be sure that infected persons were confined to house arrest, on pain of police action, there might not be a way to move beyond the "Asian mode of production" of sequestering bodies and to invent Western systems that would safeguard our digital sovereignty while also saving lives.

Lives, life.

The life that we are being urged to save by staying home and resisting the temptation of reopening.

That life is a bare one.

A life drained and depleted, as in the work of Italian philosopher Giorgio Agamben.

A life terrified of itself, gone to ground in its Kafkaesque burrow, which has become a penal colony.

A life that, in return for an assurance of survival, was ready to give up all the rest—prayer, honoring the dead, freedoms, balconies and windows from which our neighbors, once they had finished applauding the caregivers, could spy on us.

A life in which one accepts, with enthusiasm or resignation, the transformation of the welfare state into the surveillance state, with health replacing security, a life in which one consents to this slippery slope: no longer the old social contract (where you cede a bit of your individual will to gain the general will) but a new life contract (where you abdicate a little, or a lot, of your core freedoms, in return for an antivirus guarantee, an "immunity passport," a "risk-free certificate," or a new kind of get-out-of-jail-free card, one that lets you transfer to another cell). In Europe, it's a done deal. Jean-Jacques Rousseau's social contract is being slowly but surely replaced by a life contract inspired by Jeremy Bentham's utilitarianism and the "panopticon" of his surveillance state. In America, the change is on its way. Will we see Barack Obama's dream of universal healthcare overshadowed by the "army of tracers" announced by Governor Cuomo or by the Labradors trained to sniff out the coronavirus in humans?[8]

In the process, a profound break has been made with what all the wisdom of the world, notably but by no means exclusively Jewish, has striven to say: that a life is not a life if it is merely life.

That was the lesson of the Greeks from Plato to Aristotle, from the Stoics to the Epicureans and even the Cynics (I'm thinking of Diogenes in his wine barrel, who did not sound very confined when he spat out at Alexander, "You're blocking my sun!"). They all agreed that life was worthwhile only if it aspired to the good life.

It was the thinking of Nietzsche, the anti-Greek, who nevertheless agreed with the Greeks that life is never just that, and that unless it tends toward something else, unless it aspires to *great life,* unless it opens the hatches and portholes to the intelligence of other people and other things, it does not deserve to be called life.

It is the wisdom of every philosophy, truly, every one. Though they may disagree on everything else, philosophies are in accord on the idea that humanity is never identity in and for itself, never reducible to itself, but that it thrives only if–whether by action, contemplation, Spinozan effort to increase its power to be, or the divine spark–it leaves the confinement that is life in its native state.

It is the message of every human adventure.

It is the message of art.

It is the message of literature in the quest of what Sartre, in the first volume of *Situations*, called "the open road," where what is most intimate will be revealed to us in the blinding light of the city, the crowd, the world. Samuel Beckett, for his part, began *Waiting for Godot*, his portrait of humanity claustrophobically confined, with the stage direction, "A country road. A tree."

It is in opposition to all of that, in opposition to the thirst for a way forward that has been expressed by thinking and speaking humankind since books were born, that the epidemic of panic is rising up, poised atop a virus gone mad and that has driven us mad, swollen like an enormous statue of Baal erected in the middle of our emptied cities.

And it is to rebut the wisdom of the ages that a vast ad hoc team of dieticians, prophylactocrats, vegetocrats, and ecolocrats, with help from the monitors of our burrows, of our traceable dwellings governed from afar by Big Tech (which wants us to call it Alexa or Siri to lull us into a cloud in which there's no reason to consider traveling since jet fuel pollutes and one has absolutely everything – operas, symphonies, the world's greatest museums – served up digitally on the tray of an eternal breakfast in bed), is telling us, as Little Red Riding Hood was told, "Beware the open road; there lie big, bad wolves – stay home."

Well, I will say it again: we probably had no other choice, certainly not at first.

Knowing nothing about how the virus worked, governments made the right decision to suspend gatherings of the type that in Milan, Mulhouse, and New Orleans were bombs that spread terror.

And, all things considered, a heavy dose of caution, and even pandemic regulations like those in Australia authorizing visits to the beach provided one did not build sandcastles or sunbathe, or in California where one had to remain mobile on the beaches (yes to walking, running, swimming; no to sunbathing, picnics, and volleyball), are preferable to the irresponsible stupidity of the Belarussian leaders who deemed it "patriotic" not to cancel soccer matches or to Trump brazenly and blindly declaring that the country would be open for business by Easter.

But are we really sure that the changes will disappear with the pandemic?

Are we not dealing with strong trends in our societies, as announced by a multitude of early warning signs, which the pandemic is simply accentuating?

And could it be that we find ourselves confronting one of the possible forms of the much-mocked "end of history," the final sign of which Alexandre Kojève said would be the animalization of humans? Could it be that the advice to "stay home, save lives," the injunction to get used to a discount life knit together by absence, hygiene, and fear of oneself and others, also signifies this: Be like cattle in a field or, God forbid, like battery-farmed sheep destined for the slaughterhouse; be silent, barnyard animals; commune in your rediscovered animality (or vegetarianism, veganism, or veterinarianism), a realm in which the lion that was man finally lies down with the lamb? Could it be that the secular messianism sought in so much lazy thinking might finally come to roost in an animal farm?

I do not know.

What I do know is that the world after is knocking at our door and that this may be how it looks.

And, if that is the case and if, to find our road forward, we must, like Giono's hero, Angelo, go from house to house and fly from roof to roof, well, then, I know that we will have to muster our courage and go for real life, where we laugh, cry, and perhaps fall ill – but at least we will have fallen as democracy's cavalry.

CHAPTER 5

GOODBYE, WORLD?

But here, perhaps, is the worst of all.

When the pandemic was declared, I was on a mission on the Greek island of Lesbos at Moria, the camp designed for two thousand refugees but housing twenty thousand, many of whom had fled Syria into Turkey before being chased out of Turkey by Erdoğan. The refugees were crowded together in unimaginably unsanitary conditions.

And on the day the stay-at-home order was announced in France, I was on my way home from Bangladesh, a country with which I have felt a strong bond since my first visit there during its war of liberation from Pakistan in 1971. On this most recent trip, I had the occasion to verify that, fifty years down the road, the country was still a meeting point not just for every pandemic, including Covid-19, but also for every other conceivable hardship – including violent religious extremism, climate catastrophe, vast poverty, and the Rohingya refugee crisis.

Back in France, when I brought up these trips and tried to point out to the "stay home" zealots that we were dealing with two populations no less affected than we but that often lacked a home to stay in, my comments were received with icy indifference by those for whom the sole emergency was to be done with constant movement, to give nature a breather, and, in Paris, to be comfortable with ourselves and snug in our slippers.

Stranger still, when the *Wall Street Journal* and *Paris-Match* published my report from Bangladesh, which, because of the time required for writing, editing, and printing, appeared after the stay-at-home order, I watched a little wave swell on social networks (now increasingly asocial). It had the following theme: "What are you doing in the Gulf of Bengal when you should be at home? Didn't urgency or decency demand that you shelter in place like the rest of us? And even though your trip dated from before the world began to hold its breath, don't you realize that by publishing this story now you're setting an example of slackness, abandoning our joint effort, and falling short of your duty to show solidarity?"

In just a few hours, this is what I learned.

The cushy solidarity in which we are being wrapped, the upwelling of brotherhood on a Robinson Crusoe foundation of no consumption – "fewer consumer goods, more common good," go out and talk to the trees, let the light in, listen to each other – was a con.

The tide of effusion, the emissions of goodness gases purporting to crown the planet with a halo of sacrifice and abnegation, the benign energy that swirled from one satellite to the next and was ostensibly coupled, over every millimeter of the earth's crust, with a network of ethereal but durable forms of fellowship, the supposedly universal password of "let's save lives" – all that, when I had just returned, not from reporting on lives in the abstract, but on *specific* lives – those of the refugees trapped on Lesbos, those of the Bangladeshis, and those of the unemployed day laborers whom the world's new spiritual fitness regime was beginning to push out into the streets of Mexico, Cairo, and Caracas, and whose array of problems could not be summed up in the name of a virus. Yes, all that effusiveness had, as its flip side, ironclad egoism.

And as for the plan to push the pause button so as to allow the planet to breathe; as for cutting off globalization's power supply, which, according to some ecologists, the new electricity fairy was about to bring about with a wave of her ionic, renewable wand; as for bracketing and suspending the laws of the world as it was before, about which we were being lectured nonstop and for which Covid-19 would act as the circuit breaker – well, bravo! It was working! But not in the way we were told it would! Certainly not in the direction of greater equality! Because we were withdrawing from the poorest of the poor, and they were the ones who were going to pay the price of our radical generosity.

Famine was on the way. Back in my beloved Bangladesh, four in ten people had only enough food to last them three days, and the global number of people facing food crises is set to double from 135 million in 2019 to 265 million this year unless immediate humanitarian action is forthcoming. But, alas, we were well on our way to forgetting the world. It had been bothering us for ages. It had been a little dirty. We had been trying for a long time to keep it at a distance. *That,* at least, was accomplished.

* * *

I tried a simple experiment.

I went back over a week's worth of news.

No special week.

Just one particular week, and it does not matter which one because it was an ordinary week.

And I discovered that, according to the mirror that it held up to us, not a thing had happened that week except for the virus.

The migrants had disappeared.

Global warming no longer existed.

Deforestation of the Amazon, the "lung of the planet," went on as before, but no one worried about it.

The war in Yemen had not happened.

The one in Syria was a mirage.

A Nuremberg-style investigation into Syrian torture practices opened in Germany, where the henchmen of Bashar al-Assad were being tried in absentia for crimes against humanity. But it was the observance of the social-distancing measures in Baden-Württemberg that captured all the attention.

The Islamic State, which, like cellar mushrooms, grows best in the damp darkness of media distraction and first-world isolation, had come back in Iraq, with a suicide bombing in Kirkuk and ambushes in Baghdad, readying itself for a push in Rojava, and making inroads in Mozambique, where fifty young people from a village in the brush had just been slaughtered for having refused to pledge allegiance to the militant group al-Shabaab. But these events did not exist. Apart from a short dispatch here and there, they did not register.

Erdoğan, not content with having the blood of the Kurds on his hands or the squalid poverty of the refugees of Lesbos on his conscience, cut the water supply for 460,000 men, women, and children in Syrian Kurdistan just as frequent handwashing had become essential. At the same time, he was violating the territorial waters of Cyprus, a fellow member country of the European Union. He was pushing his advantage in Somalia and, as if engaged in no more than a walk in the park, sending his janissaries to stretch their legs and their Kalashnikovs in Libya. But nobody seemed too worried. Social distancing also applied between continents.

Vladimir Putin, who had swallowed the Crimea and ceded no ground in the Donbass, had not lost his sense of direction. Pursuing his dream of shattering the European Union, founded as it was on principles that he had always hated (peace, rule of law, gender equality, respect for minorities, and secularism), Putin was playing the toreador, thrusting his *banderillas* into European borders to see just how much of the unacceptable we would still accept. But Europe, or Europa, who had been a princess raised by a bull, seemed now like a blind bull, a sacrificial beast dropping its head ever lower with each thrust of the spear.

Xi Jinping, recycling the recipes of Deng Xiaoping (the color of the cat doesn't matter as long as it catches the mouse), was also taking advantage of the situation to speed up the "settlement" of the Uighur question and, in Hong Kong, to arrest opponents, persecute the free press, and lay down a "national security law" that drove the last nail into the coffin of democracy. But we only had eyes for the masks, gels, and tests that China was offering to Europe.

Viktor Orbán settled into his state of emergency. He cut subsidies to parties he did not like, to uncooperative municipalities, and to nongovernmental organizations. For this Magyar Caesar, it was no longer the Danube but the Rubicon that flowed through Budapest. The same was true in Poland, the country of Bronisław Geremek and Lech Walesa, where farcical would-be kings reminiscent of Alfred Jarry's biting 1896 play about the preposterous "King Ubu," which set the standard for the grotesque in politics, were organizing a sham of a presidential election without a campaign, without debate, and without meaningful alternatives. Not a peep from the Western media.

A democracy was emerging in Sudan. A quiet revolution continued in Algeria, the site not only of Camus's *The Plague* but also of a smiling determination among democrats that was proving stronger than the nomenklatura. Iran launched a new model of its Qased rocket, which presaged the development in the not-too-distant future of long-range missiles capable of reducing Beirut,

Riyadh, or Tel Aviv to ashes. ISIS struck Colombes, in the Paris region. In the United Kingdom, like a Golem that had slipped out of the hands of its creator, Brexit was living the good life while the prime minister was flat on his back in bed, attended by some of the immigrant physicians whom he had wanted to toss out of the country. A global recession was brewing. Food shortages loomed. In the United States, thirty million jobs vanished in a panic not seen since the 1929 crisis and the films of Frank Capra. Trump was trampling the Constitution. In typical fashion, he desecrated democracy by firing Christi A. Grimm, the principal deputy inspector general of the Department of Health and Human Services, for having sounded the alarm on critical shortages of medical supplies. Pulling dirty tricks out of his MAGA hat, he halted immigration, called on the heavily armed "good people" who had stormed Michigan's state capitol to "Liberate Michigan," spouted his usual conspiracy theories, and sank to new lows, attacking the mental health of his political rival Joe Biden. Biden was slowly but steadily gaining ground. Though his campaign was short of funds, and though social distancing led him to be compared to an "astronaut beaming back to earth from the International Space Station," he was waging war with courage and a level head.[1] In Venezuela, Nicolás Maduro, ruined by the drop in oil prices, was trying to make up for lost ground by trafficking cocaine. In Brazil, Bolsonaro was cutting entitlements and salaries and throwing the country into chaos. India was reducing its Muslims to the level of second-class citizens, while in Nigeria, Islamists continued to massacre Christians. In France, unemployment was exploding. Homeless shelters were closing. Local officials feared revolts fueled by hunger. Reaction? A whole lot of nothing. Nothing was still happening. The media had space only for theological debates on the mysteries of tocilizumab and nicotine substitutes.

The coronavirus had this virtue: that of sparing us from uninteresting, unimportant information, and relieving us of the burdens of following the vicissitudes of history, which had mercifully gone into hibernation.

And when, under the harsh light of Covid-19, we occasionally returned to the world of before (the one where we were at least a little concerned for our neighbors, for our fellow humans near and far, for Bangladesh and Lesbos), it was in that arena that we found each other most unreasonable and unaware.

April 2020? May? Like Louis XVI in his journal entry for July 14, 1789, we were all tempted to say: "Nothing."

* * *

Now, this nothingness was obviously a delusion.

The planet had continued, and continues, to spin as before.

Except that if, from one's perch on the merry-go-round, one took a view at once more elevated (vis-à-vis the world of geopolitics and the clash of views on the world) and less ironic (by conceding that it is better to live in a republic than under tyranny), one could see that the planet was spinning in the other direction.

Europe was doing the best it could. It flooded the market with liquidity. And its leaders (Emmanuel Macron, Angela Merkel, Christine Lagarde) proved worthy, standing firm against the storm and putting together a comprehensive plan for the north to support the south, for those countries best able to resist the pandemic to aid those most distressed. But we were having a great deal of difficulty resisting the advocates of retreating behind our borders. The populist wave was being held back only to gather force, it seemed, to later break the dikes and surge forth. And, when Russian aircraft loaded with masks landed in Lombardy, when the Czech Republic intercepted Chinese respirators destined for Italy, when Cuba sent urgent care specialists to a French overseas department, and when the plan to issue pooled eurobonds broke through the wall of egoism of the nations of northern Europe, you could hear the petty told-you-so crowd loudly decrying the "bankruptcy" of the "Maastricht model."

The United States sank into isolation, crippled by its viral Pearl Harbor and led by a president who had long since lost his mind but who, now, at a moment when so many lives depended on the lucidity and grip of a true commander in chief, was sorely outmatched and out of place. The trend was, in a sense, not a new one. It had begun well before Trump, of course. I devoted a book, *The Empire and the Five Kings* (2019), to America's withdrawal, to the abdication of its historic role, to the dimming of the lights of the formerly shining city on a hill.[2] Also being snuffed out was the Virgilian attempt to restart Europe as Europe had restarted Rome, which in turn had been a restart of Troy, as well as the idea that, in the course of this noble project of rebirth, one would hold high the standard of republican and democratic values; that was a delusion, too, as those values proved to be wounded eagles. Now, it seemed, we had reached the abyss. At the moment I write these lines, Donald Trump lights America on fire. He utters words that can only lead to a civil war. And, terrified by the people's rage, he entrenches himself in the White House bunker. No longer is there any question of a mission in the world or a sense of responsibility for it. America doesn't even show up for the virtual vaccine summit attended by Germany, France, Israel, the United Kingdom, Japan, and others. Not to mention Trump's promise to withdraw from the World Health Organization. Worse: for the first time in a century, the world is going through a grave crisis and yet expects nothing from the United States. Worse still: the country's enemies, which are the enemies of freedom, are crashing through the world as if America no longer counts for anything, carries no weight, no longer exists. We are entering a strange, pre-Columbian universe.

The most powerful of those enemies of freedom, Mr. Xi of China, was on the front line. While we were waging our war on the virus, he was waging another war, a real one, with the title of being the world's leading power as the prize. Chinese communism has a lot to answer for. By masking the outbreak for long weeks, manipulating statistics, intimidating whistle-blowing physicians, and imprisoning citizen journalists who posted articles on GitHub about the disastrous state of hospitals in Wuhan, the Chinese authorities helped an infection in a pangolin market mutate into a pandemic. But they engaged in the only three battles that count for a Maoist. The battle for control of names (certainly not SARS-CoV-2, which was initially proposed but sounded too much like SARS 2003 – that is, too *Chinese*). The battle for control of the story (doing everything to persuade the World Health Organization, which is subservient to the regime, to confirm that the alarm was sounded from Beijing, not from Taiwan).[3] And finally, the battle whose avatars are the "wolf warriors" of China's armed diplomacy to signal to those who have not yet caught on that the globalization of the twenty-first century will be Chinese or will not happen at all. (Some of those signals: violation of Formosa's airspace, multiplication of incidents in the East China Sea, and seizure of strategic islands and maritime zones disputed by Japan, Vietnam, the Philippines, and Brunei.) With, in addition, the tactical cunning of inventing the model response (confinement) and waiting for the adversary to adopt it before reversing course and forging ahead again.

And, as for the rest of the world, where, whatever anyone says about it, globalization had reduced poverty and increased freedom, and where, since the demise of the Soviet Union thirty years ago, people had looked west not only to see the setting sun but also to see a new sunrise; a world in which the great light of liberty was no longer rising in the east but in the west – well, that world was beginning to become resigned. Maybe the Silk Road would be better, people mused in Kabul, Bangkok, and Bujumbura, than the empire of every man for himself. Better Chinese money than a locked-down West that can see the world only in terms of corridors of contamination; a West that has a holy terror of anything that transits, expatriates, moves, and circulates; a West that speaks only of bringing its industries, talents, and capital back home. Live Chinese or die.

The world, in *Gaffiot,* the Latin dictionary from which yesterday's young people in France learned to think in French, translates as *mundus,* and it has two meanings.

First, *mundus* means the real world. The one in which people strive, grieve, hope, and die. The one that fell into ruins twice in the twentieth century – or three times, if you count the prolonged decay of communism – but that its inhabitants succeeded each time in rebuilding. The one that knows it has inherited a criminal past that, like a boa, has swallowed, and continues to swallow, all of the ancient philosophies but, despite all that, refuses to stop thinking and acting. The world, in a word, of a generation, my generation, that was raised with the conviction that it is no longer enough to watch the passing trains or to repeat, like a broken record, "never again," but that one must do everything, absolutely everything, politically, practically, actively, almost manually, to contain the "what" implied in "never again." The history of that generation has yet to be written. But such was its sensible arrogance. Such was its new philosophy. Its masters were not Karl Marx or Carl Schmitt, but gentler philosophers (Emmanuel Levinas); its masters were somber but committed souls who had fought the beast with bare hands (the International Brigades in Spain, Ernest Hemingway, André Malraux). And they were, in our eyes, the most admirable of men because they were both present in the world and present in words, combining the art of the fighter with that of the poet. And because their world was buried up to its neck in its death instinct and totalitarian memory, our masters gave us the weapons and the tools, not to remake it, but to repair it. It was under their hand that we went to Biafra, to the Vietnamese boat people, to Bangladesh. And it was thanks to them that we saw, as if in a crystal ball, the twin villainy of accepting the status quo and pretending to "cure" it. We took to the road. I went to Cambodia with Joan Baez, to Sarajevo at the same time as Susan Sontag. It was in the school of those masters that "human rightsism" and "without borderism" were invented. And in that there is nothing to be ashamed of.

But *mundus* also signifies what is neat and clean. Immaculate and without stain. Aseptic. Sanitized. Disinfected. In Greek, the word is *cosmos*. In French and English, *cosmetic*. And it is the name of another world, one unconcerned about and forgetful of its accursed and appalling side, which it is our human task to confront. It is the name of a too beautiful world in which we are asked to hide the misery, the evil, the Medusas that we would prefer not to see. In that world, which is as old as the other world but has just had its image restored by the coronavirus, people who travel by plane to report on what is happening in the Gulf of Bengal are endangering the planet. Internationalists who travel to regions of the world where the grim reaper eclipses all other names and places are sticking their noses where they don't belong and should come home. And, upon their return, what do the travelers find? A world over which reign ventilation technicians, the supervisors-in-chief of the state of emergency, death-agony assistants. A world where, instead of the one that hurts too much, we have hydroalcoholic sanitizing gels, balconies from which we compliment ourselves, dogs to walk twice a day while carrying one's

Covid-19 certificate, and cities purged of their crowds like an operating room purged of its nosocomial infections. A world of dog-masters – that is, masters who are dogs and train a race of beings that has the right only to bark when reminded that it is made up of people, to whine when it catches a virus, and to yap when Corona, our king, arrives to give us its lesson, using carrots and sticks. The world is made for us to huddle up in, says King Corona. It is made to lie down in. And if sleep is slow in coming, one must count sheep, or one's money, if one has any, or one's viruses.

Life isn't beautiful yet?

Can't we get everything we need with a couple of clicks – basic necessities but also, ultimately, sex, imagination, death? Remember the other meaning of *mundus* . . . clean, neat, tidy, and, as we say in French, *net.*

That is the lesson of the virus.

That is the reason for my anger.

And that is why it was important to resist the wind of madness blowing over the world.

NOTES

PROLOGUE

1. TOI Staff, "Hamas Chief Threatens Israel over Ventilators for Coronavirus Patients," *Times of Israel*, April 2, 2020, https://www.timesofisrael.com /hamas-chief-threatens-israel-over-ventilators-for -coronavirus-patients/.
2. "Nigeria Security Forces Kill 18 Over Virus Lockdown: Rights Body," AFP, April 16, 2020, https://www.barrons.com/news/18-killed-by -nigeria-security-forces-over-virus-lockdown-rights -body-01587037505.
3. "President Trump Tweets: 'LIBERATE MICHIGAN!'" Fox 2 Detroit, April 17, 2020, https://www.fox2detroit.com /news/president-trump-tweets-liberate-michigan.

CHAPTER 1:
COME BACK, MICHEL FOUCAULT—WE NEED YOU!

1. Michael Specter, "How Anthony Fauci Became America's Doctor," *New Yorker*, April 10, 2020, https://www.newyorker.com/magazine/2020/04/20/how-anthony-fauci-became-americas-doctor.
2. Frank Bruni, "She Predicted the Coronavirus: What Does She See Next?," *New York Times*, May 2, 2020, https://www.nytimes.com/2020/05/02/opinion/sunday/coronavirus-prediction-laurie-garrett.html; David Ewing Duncan, "'Prepare, Prepare, Prepare': Why Didn't the World Listen to the Coronavirus Cassandras?" *Vanity Fair*, March 27, 2020, https://www.vanityfair.com/news/2020/03/why-didnt-the-world-listen-to-the-coronavirus-cassandras.
3. Mehmet Oz ("Dr. Oz"), interview by Sean Hannity, *Hannity*, Fox News Channel, April 16, 2020, https://www.youtube.com/watch?v=zkwpHKb0ZFU; Emily Yahr, "The Long and Winding Evolution of Dr. Drew, Back in the Spotlight after a Coronavirus Controversy," *Washington Post*, April 13, 2020, https://www.washingtonpost.com/arts-entertainment/2020/04/13/dr-drew-pinsky-coronavirus-loveline/ (video of Drew Pinsky's comments available at https://twitter.com

/droopsdr/status/1246104168655466498?lang=en); and Phil McGraw ("Dr. Phil"), interview by Laura Ingraham, *The Ingraham Angle,* Fox News Channel, April 16, 2020, https://www.youtube.com/watch?v=5GLwsH8EwgA.

4. Mathieu Lecerf, "Didier Raoult, 'le Gérard Depardieu de la science': le médecin fascine et intrigue," *Gala,* March 26, 2020, https://www.gala.fr/l_actu/news_de_stars/didier-raoult-le-gerard-depardieu-de-la-science-le-medecin-fascine-et-intrigue_445549. See the masterpieces of the history of science by my professor and mentor Georges Canguilhem: *Le Normal et le pathologique* (1966; Paris: Presses Universitaires de France, 2013) and *La Formation du concept de réflexe aux XVII*[e] *et XVIII*[e] *siècles* (Paris: Presses Universitaires de France, 1955).
5. Isabelle Cavé, *Les Médecins-législateurs et le mouvement hygiéniste sous la Troisième République* (Physician-Legislators and the Hygienic Movement under the Third Republic in France).
6. Quoted in Xavier de Jarcy, *Les Abandonnés: Histoire des "cités de banlieue"* (Paris: Albin Michel, 2019).
7. Alain Drouard, *Une Inconnue des sciences sociales: La Fondation Alexis Carrel, 1941–1945* (Paris: Éditions de la Maison des Sciences de l'Homme, 1992) xiv,

wherein a footnote attributes it to R.-H. Guerrand, 1987, "Henri Sellier et le service social, *Colloque Henri Sellier et les cites-jardins,* mars 1983, Presses universitaires de Vincennes.

8. Anne-Charlotte Dusseaulx, "Coronavirus: voici ceux qui devront rester confinés après le 11 mai, selon le conseil scientifique," *Le Journal du Dimanche,* April 15, 2020, https://www.lejdd.fr/Societe/coronavirus-voici-ceux-qui-devront-rester-confines-apres-le-11-mai-selon-le-conseil-scientifique-3962147.

CHAPTER 2: DIVINE SURPRISE

1. Henry de Montherlant, "La paix dans la guerre" (Ides et calendes, Neuchâtel, 1941); Paul Morand, *Chroniques, 1931–1954* (Paris: Grasset, 2001).
2. André Gide, *Journals,* Vol. 4: 1939–1949 (Urbana: University of Illinois Press), 39; Albert Camus, *The Plague* (1947; New York: Vintage, 1991), 97, 94.
3. Steven Erlanger, "Spread of Virus Could Hasten the Great Coming Apart of Globalization," *New York Times,* February 25, 2020, https://www.nytimes.com/2020/02/25/world/europe/coronavirus-globalization-backlash.html; Jacques Lacan, "Entretien au magazine *Panorama,* 1974," *La Cause*

Du Désir 88, no. 3 (2014): 165–173, https://www.cairn.info/revue-la-cause-du-desir-2014-3.htm.

4. David Quammen, "We Made the Coronavirus Epidemic," *New York Times*, January 28, 2020, https://www.nytimes.com/2020/01/28/opinion/coronavirus-china.html; Damian Carrington, "Coronavirus: 'Nature Is Sending Us a Message,' Says UN Environment Chief," *Guardian*, March 25, 2020, https://www.theguardian.com/world/2020/mar/25/coronavirus-nature-is-sending-us-a-message-says-un-environment-chief; and Tyler McCarthy, "Michael Moore Says Coronavirus Is a Warning Before Earth Gets 'Revenge' Over Climate Change," Fox News, https://www.foxnews.com/entertainment/michael-moore-coronavirus-warning-earth-revenge-climate-change.
5. Yves Citton, "Panique virale: comment ne pas rater la catastrophe?," AOC, April 7, 2020, https://aoc.media/analyse/2020/04/06/panique-virale-comment-ne-pas-rater-la-catastrophe/.
6. Mark Lawrence Schrad ("a new kind of patriotism"), Peter T. Coleman ("a decline in polarization"), Archon Fung ("a new civic federalism"), Sherry Turkle ("a healthier digital lifestyle"), and Paul Freedman ("more cooking"), "Coronavirus Will

Change the World Permanently. Here's How," *Politico,* March 19, 2020, https://www.politico.com/news/magazine/2020/03/19/coronavirus-effect-economy-life-society-analysis-covid-135579.

7. Citton, "Panique virale."
8. Carrington, "Coronavirus"; Nicolas Hulot, "Nous recevons une sorte d'ultimatum de la nature," interview by Apolline de Malherbe, BFMTV, March 22, 2020, https://www.bfmtv.com/mediaplayer/video/nicolas-hulot-nous-recevons-une-sorte-d-ultimatum-de-la-nature-1232518.html.
9. Bruno Latour, "Imaginer les gestes-barrières contre le retour à la production d'avant-crise," AOC, March 30, 2020, https://aoc.media/opinion/2020/03/29/imaginer-les-gestes-barrieres-contre-le-retour-a-la-production-davant-crise/.
10. Lee Brown, "Evangelical Pastor Claims Coronavirus Is God's 'Death Angel' to 'Purge a Lot of Sin,'" *New York Post*, January 29, 2020, https://nypost.com/2020/01/29/evangelical-pastor-claims-coronavirus-is-gods-death-angel-to-purge-a-lot-of-sin/; Jean-François Jacobs, "Dieu est tout-puissant . . . mais le coronavirus l'est encore plus!" ASBL, April 25, 2020, https://www.athees.net/category/religion/; Christine Boutin, Twitter post, March

19, 2020, https://twitter.com/christineboutin/status/1240557512107188224.

11. "Fornication et adultère ont créé le coronavirus, selon le frère de Tariq Ramadan," *Le Point*, March 22, 2020, https://www.lepoint.fr/monde/fornication-et-adultere-ont-cree-le-coronavirus-selon-le-frere-de-tariq-ramadan-22-03-2020-2368185_24.php.
12. Camus, *The Plague*, 98.
13. Jean de La Fontaine, "The Animals Sick of the Plague," *The Original Fables of La Fontaine*, trans. F. C. Tilney (Urbana: Project Gutenberg, 2005), Book VII, Fable 1, https://www.gutenberg.org/ebooks/15946; "Une démonologie populaire se forme sous nos yeux sur les réseaux sociaux," Conspiracy Watch, March 25, 2020, https://www.conspiracywatch.info/taguieff-une-demonologie-populaire-se-forme-sous-nos-yeux-sur-les-reseaux-sociaux.html; Walter Russell Mead, "Amid the Pandemic, Anti-Semitism Flares Up," *Wall Street Journal*, April 15, 2020, https://www.wsj.com/articles/amid-the-pandemic-anti-semitism-flares-up-11586991224.
14. David L. Katz, "Is Our Fight Against Coronavirus Worse Than the Disease?" *New York Times*, March 20, 2020, https://www.nytimes.com/2020/03/20/opinion/coronavirus-pandemic-social-distancing.html.

15. Thomas L. Friedman, "A Plan to Get America Back to Work," *New York Times,* March 22, 2020, https://www.nytimes.com/2020/03/22/opinion/coronavirus-economy.html; Editorial Board, "The Economic Lockdown Catastrophe," *Wall Street Journal,* May 8, 2020, https://www.wsj.com/articles/the-economic-lockdown-catastrophe-11588978716.
16. Jacques Lacan, "Freud pour toujours: entretien avec Jacques Lacan" (translated from the Italian by P. Lemoine), *Magazine littéraire* 428 (2004) [1974]: 28.

CHAPTER 3: DELICIOUS CONFINEMENT

1. "Dr. Anthony Fauci on How Life Returns to Normal," interview by Kate Linebaugh, April 7, 2020, in *The Journal, Wall Street Journal* podcast, https://www.wsj.com/podcasts/the-journal/dr-anthony-fauci-on-how-life-returns-to-normal/d5754969-7027-431e-89fa-e12788ed9879.
2. Pirkei Avot, 1:14.
3. Florence Richter, "Jean Genet, poète et voyou," *Revue interdisciplinaire d'études juridiques* 61, no. 2 (2008): 73–89; Jean Genet, *Miracle of the Rose* (1946; New York: Grove Press, 1994), 31.
4. René Crevel, "Mort, maladie et littérature," *Le*

Surréalisme au service de la revolution, no. 1, July 1930.

CHAPTER 4: LIFE, THEY SAY

1. Alan Feuer, Ashley Southall, and Michael Gold, “Dozens of Decomposing Bodies Found in Trucks at Brooklyn Funeral Home,” *New York Times,* April 29, 2020, https://www.nytimes.com/2020/04/29/nyregion/bodies-brooklyn-funeral-home-coronavirus.html.
2. Dave Goldiner, “Cuomo Calls Nursing Homes a ‘Feeding Frenzy’ for Coronavirus as 540 Die in New York,” *New York Daily News,* April 18, 2020, https://www.nydailynews.com/coronavirus/ny-coronavirus-cuomo-20200418-jqd6ojzmazdupla7zzj5laraky-story.html; Jon Kamp and Anna Wilde Mathews, “As U.S. Nursing-Home Deaths Reach 50,000, States Ease Lockdowns,” *Wall Street Journal,* June 16, 2020, https://www.wsj.com/articles/coronavirus-deaths-in-u-s-nursing-long-term-care-facilities-top-50-000-11592306919.
3. “Coronavirus: ‘40 à 50% des patients meurent’ en réanimation, selon le Dr Karine Lacombe,” interview by Jean-Jacques Bourdin, BFM, April 13, 2020,

https://www.bfmtv.com/sante/coronavirus-40-a-50-percent-des-patients-meurent-en-reanimation-selon-le-dr-karine-lacombe-1892706.html; Véronique Fournier, "Covid-19: la réa jusqu'à quel âge?" *Libération,* April 27, 2020, https://www.liberation.fr/debats/2020/04/27/covid-19-la-rea-jusqu-a-quel-age_1786560.

4. Palmer Haasch, "Gaming Companies Are Inserting WHO Coronavirus Guidance into Games in an Effort to Encourage Players to Stay Home," *Insider,* March 30, 2020, https://www.insider.com/play-apart-together-who-coronavirus-covid-19-blizzard-riot-twitch-2020-3.
5. Natasha Singer, "Employers Rush to Adopt Virus Screening. The Tools May Not Help Much," *New York Times,* May 11, 2020, https://www.nytimes.com/2020/05/11/technology/coronavirus-worker-testing-privacy.html.
6. Mike Giglio, "Would You Sacrifice Your Privacy to Get Out of Quarantine?" *Atlantic,* April 22, 2020, https://www.theatlantic.com/politics/archive/2020/04/coronavirus-pandemic-privacy-civil-liberties-911/609172/; Kirsten Grind, Robert McMillan, and Anna Wilde Mathews, "To Track Virus, Governments Weigh Surveillance Tools That

Push Privacy Limits," *Wall Street Journal,* March 17, 2020, https://www.wsj.com/articles/to-track-virus-governments-weigh-surveillance-tools-that-push-privacy-limits-11584479841.

7. Sara Dorn, "De Blasio's Social Distancing Hotline Sending Cops on Thousands of Bogus Calls," *New York Post,* April 25, 2020, https://nypost.com/2020/04/25/social-distancing-complaints-sending-cops-on-dead-end-calls/.
8. Shan Li, "New York to Hire 'Army of Tracers' to Combat Coronavirus," *Wall Street Journal,* April 30, 2020, https://www.wsj.com/articles/new-york-to-hire-army-of-tracers-to-combat-coronavirus-11588276752; Karin Brulliard, "Dogs Are Being Trained to Sniff Out Coronavirus Cases," *Washington Post,* April 29, 2020, https://www.washingtonpost.com/science/2020/04/29/coronavirus-detection-dogs/.

CHAPTER 5: GOODBYE, WORLD?

1. David Axelrod and David Plouffe, "What Joe Biden Needs to Do to Beat Trump," *New York Times,* May 4, 2020, https://www.nytimes.com/2020/05/04/opinion/axelrod-plouffe-joe-biden.html.

2. Bernard-Henri Lévy, *The Empire and the Five Kings: America's Abdication and the Fate of the World* (New York: Henry Holt, 2019).
3. Paul Benkimoun, Frédéric Lemaître, et Marie Bourreau, "Les liaisons dangereuses entre l'OMS et la Chine ont marqué la crise du coronavirus," April 27, 2020, https://www.lemonde.fr/international/article/2020/04/27/les-liaisons-dangereuses-entre-l-oms-et-la-chine-ont-marque-la-crise-du-coronavirus_6037929_3210.html.